# PREHISTORIC ASTRONOMY
# IN THE SOUTHWEST

## REVISED EDITION

## J. McKIM MALVILLE
## CLAUDIA PUTNAM

Johnson Books: Boulder

## Dedication

We dedicate this book to the community of Yellow Jacket within whose midst scores of students and faculty from the University of Colorado have lived and worked for more than three decades of summer archaeology.

**Library of Congress Cataloging-in-Publication Data**
  J. McKim Malville
    Prehistoric astronomy in the Southwest / J. McKim Malville, Claudia Putnam. —2nd ed.
      p.     cm.
    Includes bibliographical references and index.
    ISBN 1-55566-116-5
    1. Indians of North America—Southwest,  New—Astronomy.
2. Astronomy, Prehistoric—Southwest,  New.   3. Indians of North America—Southwest,  New—Antiquities.   4. Southwest, New—Antiquities.   I. Putnam, Claudia.   II. Title.
E78.S7M135   1993
522'.0979—dc20                                                    93-17712
                                                                      CIP

Cover design:  Ann Dowden
Cover photograph: J. McKim Malville. Moonrise on the morning of August 8, 1988. The moon's declination was 28.5°. The bright stars rising ahead of the moon were $\phi$ Aurigae and $\beta$ Tauri (El Nath). The rising of the moon between the chimneys is visible from the Chimney Rock Pueblo only at the times of major northern standstill occurring every 18.61 years.

Printed in the United States of America by
Johnson Printing Company
1880 South 57th Court
Boulder, Colorado 80301

# Contents

# Acknowledgements

Our first introduction to the possibilities of astronomy at Yellow Jacket was provided by Mark Neupert in the summer of 1986. Since then we have received much appreciated encouragement and advice from Dr. Joe Ben Wheat, Dr. Frank Eddy, and Dr. Frederick Lange. Hardworking field research teams, who have fought the gnats and sage with determination and good humor, have included Dr. Carol Ambruster, Ken Brownsberger, John Cater, John Jacobs, Annie Jones, Jean Kindig, Matt Moody, Rudy Poglitsh, Jennifer Ritter, Jim Walton, and Cindy Webb. The surveying equipment has been generously loaned by Milan Halek of the Civil Engineering Department at the University of Colorado. Financial aid for the field work has been provided by the Councils for Research and Creative Work, Outreach, and Teaching, and by the Undergraduate Research Opportunity Program of the University of Colorado. We thank the Wilson family and the Archaeological Conservancy for permission to work on their lands at Yellow Jacket. We are indebted to Dale Lightfoot for his map of Chimney Rock and to Jean Kindig for her many fine drawings throughout the book.

For the new material in this second edition on the astronomy of the Sun Temple and Cliff Palace of Mesa Verde, we gratefully acknowledge the permission and support of Superintendent Robert C. Heyder, Chief Ranger Howard Dimont, and Jack Smith, former Chief of Research and Resource Management. Considerable assistance in the field was provided by Frank Occhipinti, Greg Munson, Aaron Kaye, Don Ross, and Kelley Shepherd.

# One

## The Anasazi Astronomer

*When a child was born his Corn Mother was placed beside him, where it was kept for twenty days, and during this period he was kept in darkness. . . Early on the morning of the twentieth day, the mother holding the child in her left arm and the Corn Mother in her right hand, and accompanied by her own mother—the child's grandmother—left the house and walked to the east. Then they stopped, facing east, and prayed silently, casting pinches of cornmeal to the rising sun. When the sun cleared the horizon the mother stepped forward, held up the child to the sun, and said, 'Father Sun, this is your child.'* [1]

Above the rim of the horizon the deep blue extends to the edge of space. For many people, the blue of the overarching sky means infinity, mystery, and power. The sky is peopled with gods: sky gods, sun gods, wind gods, rain gods. Gods threw thunderbolts, carried the sun from east to west, protected it from hungry demons. The first astronomers of our planet attended to the needs of these deities. They were servants and priests to mystery and power.

The science of astronomy has taken many forms over the past five thousand years, always strongly reflecting the culture in which it was embedded. An extraordinary variety of institutions and practices has arisen to support this science, the oldest of all, in vastly different environments around the world.

Today's astronomers are physicists who seek to understand the light of distant stars and galaxies in terms of fundamental physical phenomena that occur on the earth. But we do more, for astronomers explore the fabric of time. With telescopes as our shovels, we dig back to our origins using the ancient photons of the universe. The cosmologists of today are asking the questions asked for millennia as people, sitting around a campfire at night, wondered about the meaning of those flickering but eternal stars overhead and the fragile, transient life around us.

In the sub-field of astronomy known as archaeoastronomy, the challenge is to "get under the skin" of those ancient sky watchers and to be able see the heavens through their eyes. The astronomers who preceded us knew their heavens and their stars: the Anasazi sun watchers, the court astrologers of Peking and Babylon, the astronomer kings of Copan and Palenque, the astronomer architects of the great temples of India and the stone circles of Great Britain, and even the blood encrusted astronomer priests of the Aztec capital of Tenochtitlán. Why did they go to so much effort to align their cities and temples and assimilate their lives to a perceived cosmic order?

Not only were these astronomers driven by their own curiosity about the natural world and its cycles of time, but they also served the needs of the societies in which they lived. They advised emperors and generals, attempted to predict eclipses and conjunctions of planets, devised calendars for festivals and established dates for planting. Sometimes overtly or sometimes subtly, these ancient astronomers provided authority and legitimacy for their emperors and kings.

Astronomers have used a variety of techniques for preserving and transmitting knowledge. Today, in western science we have lectures, scientific journals, and professional meetings. In the past, other cultures used a rich variety of techniques in addition to the written word: folk stories, myths, elaborate rituals and festivals, complex and symbolic architecture, dance, and costumes. The Anasazi have left us their sacred spaces, the organized rocks of architecture, and markings on canyon walls as records of their astronomy.

Those stones with which people have built their homes and temples can be transmitters of information about their innermost thoughts as well as information about the details of their astronomical knowledge. The structure of the temples of India, for example, provide insights about the beliefs of a people concerning the nature and origin of their world.[2] In their stones are encoded the myths of innumerable gods and demons, many of whom were responsible in one way or another for the creation of the world. Deep in their dark centers lies the *garbha griha*, the "womb chamber," symbolic of the powerful and dangerous chaos out of which our world developed. The center of the temple also represents a cave in the cosmic mountain, the axis of the world connecting heaven and earth. It is to this center that the devout Hindu returns periodically for worship and rejuvenation. The devotee will often enter the temple compound through a doorway opening to the east. In some temples of southern India, the rays of the rising sun at equinox sweep through long passageways into the sacred center and touch the image of the god enshrined therein.

The great temple, the Templo Mayor, at the center of the Aztec capital of Tenochtitlán, is another structure which informs us of the origin myths and the social customs of the Mexica.[3] The Templo Mayor represents the primordial mountain of the Aztecs, the Serpent Mountain of Coatapec. On its flanks the first battle between the forces of light and darkness took place. The god of the sun, Huitzilopochtli was victorious, killing and dismembering the moon goddess, Coyolxuahqui. The stone of Coyolxuahqui, 11 feet across, lies at the base of the Templo Mayor, near the Cathedral of Mexico City, bearing witness to the great cosmogonic duel. On that temple, with the great drum sounding and conch shells and horns blowing, that initial battle was re-enacted in the form of human sacrifice. The Templo Mayor had apparently been oriented so that on the morning of equinox the sun would first appear between its twin towers.

The Anasazi were one of three major agricultural groups of the prehistoric Southwest. The other two, the Mogollon and the Hohokam, lived to the south of the Anasazi. The Mogollon may have been the first to cultivate plants. The Hohokam developed a cultural network similar in sophistication to Chaco Canyon. They are known for their extensive canal systems and ball courts. The most comprehensive knowledge of prehistoric astronomy in the Southwest comes from studies of the Anasazi, and it is upon that culture that we focus our attention.

Since the first printing of this book in the spring of 1989, there have been four summers of field work and a steady increase in our knowledge of Anasazi astronomy. Four years ago we had identified four major Anasazi sites that evidenced astronomical activity,[4] but the most famous of all Southwestern archaeological sites, Mesa Verde, was strangely absent from the group. Now it joins the others,[5] and this second edition contains a new chapter describing some of the recent discoveries of astronomy at Mesa Verde.

The ancient people of the American Southwest lived close to the heavens and paid attention to what was overhead. The average Anasazi must have had a better knowledge of the patterns of the stars and cycles of sun and moon than the average inhabitant of the Southwest today. A thousand years ago people's lives were governed by the intertwining cycles of sun and moon, and observational astronomy must have played major roles in providing planting and ritual calendars.

We can trace in broad strokes the likely development and flow of Anasazi astronomy during the four centuries from approximately A.D. 900 to A.D. 1300. Chaco Canyon was clearly the center of a major spurt of astronomical activity. There are moments in history when life accelerates, new ideas flash into people's minds, and great works are created.

The Bonito Phase of Chaco Canyon appears to have been such a time when extraordinary architecture was constructed and the cycles of the heavens were perceived and utilized by sharp-eyed observers. By providing dates for rituals, festivals, and pilgrimages, astronomical knowledge may have been one of the sources of social cohesion which tied the far-flung Chacoan society together.[6] The Chacoan community at Chimney Rock could have provided important calendrical information.[7] Other outliers may have contributed to the growth of astronomical knowledge in ways we do not yet understand. With the fading of the power of Chaco Canyon in the early years of the 12th century, there appears to have been a movement of leadership northward to the outliers of Salmon and Aztec. Then, later in the 12th century, the focus of activity moved further north of the San Juan into the Montezuma Basin. Information is easily transported, and the populations of the major settlements in the area, such as Yellow Jacket, Mesa Verde, and Hovenweep, may have inherited some of the astronomical knowledge of the previous centuries.

The evidence for observational astronomy that we present in this book provides a fascinating glimpse into the manner in which the early Americans of the Southwest integrated their lives into the larger cosmos and adapted to difficult and uncertain environments. As we encounter more examples of their knowledge of astronomy, two questions keep returning to tantalize and challenge us: how did the Anasazi make their astronomical observations, which were sometimes remarkably precise, and why did they appear to expend so much effort on astronomy?

Ethnographic analogy is one approach to pursuing these issues. The presence of similar objects or architectural structures in both living and prehistoric cultures may indicate similar function and meaning. But as one reaches further back in time the legitimacy of such inference diminishes and assumptions of similarity become more suspect. As it has been developed by the archaeologist Lewis Binford ethnographic analogy is used as a strategy to generate hypotheses and models that can be tested.[8] Producing neither proofs nor firm answers, ethnographic analogy primarily provides a focus for further field studies. The discovery of an astronomical sight-line, for example, is thus not an end in itself, but should be the inspiration for new investigations that result ultimately in increased understanding of people and their culture.

# *Two*

# The Dome of the Sky

Our experience of time on this planet comes from the two major motions of the earth, one its spinning on its axis and the other its annual revolution around the sun. The spinning earth gives us clock time, sunrises and sunsets, and all those experiences of temperature changes and habits of sleep associated with night and day. The motion of the earth in its orbit around the sun provides us with calendrical time. It gives us birthdays, the seasons, the heat of summer, and the cold of winter. Driven by these two motions of the earth in space, the sun traces a daily as well as seasonally changing path across the sky.

Events in the sky, whether by day or by night, appear to occur on the inside surface of a vast hemispherical screen. The early Greeks imagined the sky to be a series of spheres composed of indestructible crystalline material with stars embedded like small bright jewels. Using the wheel as a metaphor for the heavens, they imagined that the spheres rotated, with the earth at the unmoving center. The Greeks recognized that the sphere of stars had to lie at a great distance from the earth, because the stars did not change their positions as sky watchers moved across the surface of the earth.

Cultures that did not possess the wheel, such as those of Mesoamerica, divided the heavens above and the worlds below into parallel layers. The Pueblo cultures of the American Southwest have an intermediate cosmology consisting of layers of hemispheres. Beneath our world lie three or four dome-like worlds through which their ancestors passed in their struggle upward.

At one time of the night we see only a half-sphere over our head. But given time and patience enough, watching new stars rise in the east and old ones set in the west, we sense that there is a full sphere of stars surrounding us and that we lie at its center. Each of us seems to be at the center of a vast and slowly turning sphere of stars.

Unfamiliar and often confusing to us city dwellers, the paths of the stars and sun across the hemispherical sky must have been familiar and predictable to ancient sky watchers. Part of our amazement over the accomplishments of ancient astronomers results from our own night blindness, from our inability to see the skies in our brightly lit and building-enclosed world.

The sky is one of the major symbols in the natural world of order and cyclic repetition. Yet the translucent blue of the sky seems infinitely distant and the gods living there infinitely inaccessible. In many cultures, people have transformed their homes and temples into miniature universes, which are smaller and more manageable than the larger reality. The circular kiva of the Pueblo, the hogan of the Navajo, the dome of the Indian stupa and Tibetan chorten, and even the dome of St. Peter's mimic the celestial sphere.

## The Kiva as an Astronomical Symbol

Ever mysterious in her cycles of life and death, in her power to provide life and then take it away, Mother Nature is an inscrutable benefactress: not always benign nor fully predictable. To the Anasazi living along the northern frontier, the world must have often been threatening and dangerous. Especially during periods of climatic instability, agriculture would have been unpredictable and frustrating. Sometimes the growing season may have been so short that the crops yielded little food. The animals may have been strangely absent. The anticipated rains may never have arrived. Overlying this uncertain life, moving smoothly and confidently across the sky, the regularity of the sun was in clear conflict with the uncertain chaos of the land beneath.

It was such a distinction between the apparent unchanging order of the heavens and the painful change and decay of the earth that led Plato and Aristotle to separate the two realms. The four elements of the Greeks—air, fire, earth, and water—moved with straight line motion on the earth; the fifth crystalline element, aether, moved in endless circular motion in the heavens. The Anasazi may have adopted another strategy to deal with the conflict between heaven and earth, building circular kivas as copies of the heavens. With a dome overhead, aligned to the four cardinal points of space, the microcosm of the kiva may have been a place to achieve harmony with the larger world.

The kiva is the most characteristic feature of Pueblo and Anasazi architecture (Figure 1). Like the sacred structures of India and Mexico, as well as others around the world, it provides both a cosmology and a cosmogony, a description of the world as it is and a theory of how the world came into being. According to modern Pueblo tradition, the kiva represents the *sipapu*, the place where the first humans emerged from the lower worlds.[1]

**Anasazi kivas, looking south (photographed with a 14mm lens)**

**Figure 1a.** Great Kiva of Casa Rinconada. The typical great kiva contained a raised fire box, raised oblong floor vaults placed between the supports for the roof columns, and a north ground level room reached by a staircase.

**Figure 1b.** Kiva at Yellow Jacket, 5MT-2. The characteristic features of kivas of the northern Anasazi are a sipapu, hearth, deflector stone, southern recess, and six pilasters along the perimeter.

*When they built the kiva, they first put up beams of four different trees.*
*These were the trees that were planted in the underworld for the people to*
*climb up on. In the north, under the foundation they placed yellow turquoise;*
*in the west, blue turquoise, in the south, red, and in the east, white turquoise.*
*Prayer sticks are placed at each place so the foundation will be strong and will*
*never give way. The walls represent the sky; the beams of the roof (made of*
*wood of the first four trees) represent the Milky Way. The sky looks like a cir-*
*cle, hence the round shape of the kiva.*[2]

Itself a symbolic point of emergence of the ancestors, the kiva may
also contain a *sipapu* in its floor, slightly north of center. The four pillars
of the Anasazi great kiva may have represented the trees planted in the
underworld or the four sacred mountains. The kiva thereby may have
been a cosmological link between heaven and earth as well as a cosmogonic link between past and present.[3]

In Chaco Canyon, many kivas in Pueblo Bonito had cribbed roofs
made of horizontal logs placed at regular intervals along low benches.
As many as 350 pine logs were used in the kiva roofs, most if not all of
which had been carried or dragged over large distances.[4] Kivas range
in diameter from 10 feet to over 60 feet as is the case of the great kivas
at Yellow Jacket and Casa Rinconada in Chaco Canyon.[5] The amount
of labor needed to construct these primarily subterranean great kivas
was enormous and indicates the great importance the Anasazi gave to
the construction of ceremonial buildings. In the Great Kiva of Casa
Rinconada, the four pillars supporting the roof were carefully aligned
to the four cardinal directions[6] (Figure 2). Precision of orientation appeared necessary to achieve a suitable copy of the sky.

## Azimuth and Altitude

In order to identify the position of the sun or of a star on the celestial
sphere, we use two coordinates, azimuth and altitude. The azimuth of a
star is its position along the horizon, measured clockwise in degrees
from the north. Altitude is the distance, measured in degrees, upward
from the horizon toward the zenith (Figure 3). The altitude of a star
just on the horizon is 0°; a star which is directly overhead has an altitude of 90°.

We measure the sky by degrees, minutes, and seconds. The separa-
tion of the two stars of the Big Dipper is 5°. At arm's length, an out-
stretched adult hand, from extended thumb to little finger is about 18°;
one's finger tip appears approximately 1° across. The sun and moon
have diameters of 0.5°.

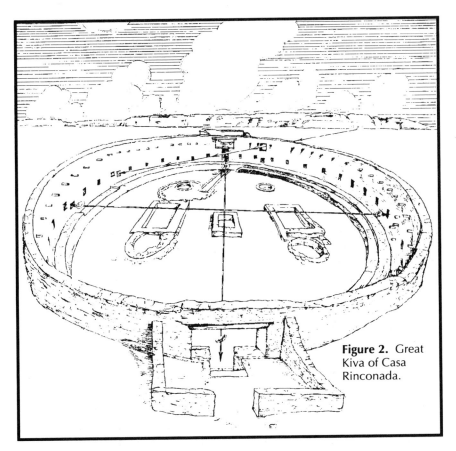

**Figure 2.** Great Kiva of Casa Rinconada.

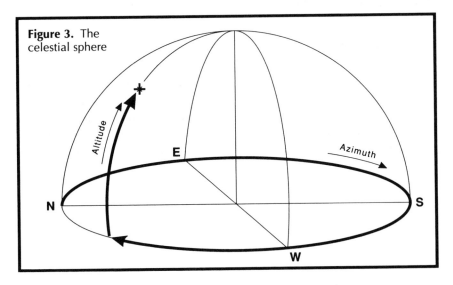

**Figure 3.** The celestial sphere

Because the measurement of azimuth always starts at the north, the azimuth of the North Pole point in the sky is always 0°, as viewed everywhere on the earth. But the altitude of the North Star varies with our location on the earth. At the North Pole, the North Star is almost directly overhead, with an altitude of 90°. At the equator it lies on the horizon and its altitude is thus 0° (Figure 4).

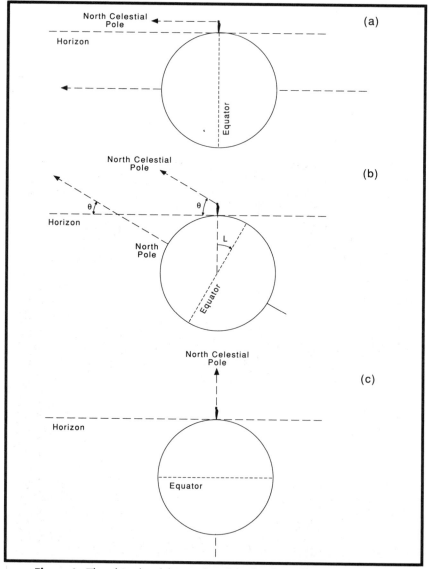

**Figure 4.** The altitude of the north celestial pole at different latitudes.

At any particular place, the altitude of the North Star equals the latitude of that location. As one travels from the North Pole to the equator, the North Star thus falls in the sky from the zenith to the northern horizon. At the equator of the earth with a latitude of 0°, the altitude of the North Star is also 0°. At Yellow Jacket with a latitude of 37.5°, the pole of the heavens lies 37.5° above the northern horizon.

## The Pole Star

The earth rotates on its axis in a counter-clockwise direction as seen from above the North Pole of the earth. Due to that rotation, the stars appear to move from east to west across the celestial sphere. In one hour the sun will move approximately 15°. There is a special set of stars, known as circumpolar stars, which are sufficiently close to the north polar point that they never sink below the northern horizon and hence are visible on any night of the year (Figure 5).

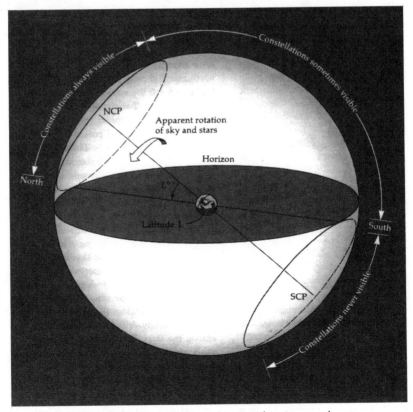

**Figure 5.** The celestial sphere showing the circumpolar stars

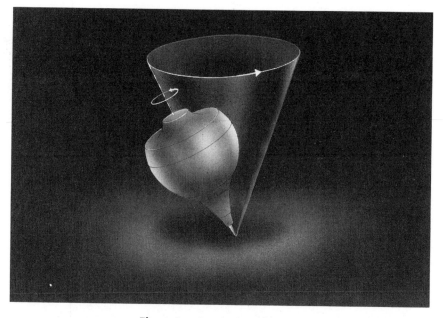

**Figure 6a.** Precession of a top.

**Figure 6b.** Precession of the earth.

The North Star, Polaris, is today one of these circumpolar stars. But it has not always been so, nor have we humans always had a North Star with which to guide our travels or align our buildings. Even today it is not precisely at the north polar point but lies slightly less than a degree away.

The axis of the earth wobbles, like that of a spinning top, slowly changing the direction to which it points on the celestial sphere. That slow wobble, which takes 26,000 years, is known as precession (Figure 6). As a result of the wobbles, the north polar point slowly sweeps through the sky. During most of the past, there has been no bright star near the north polar point, just as there is no bright star currently near the south polar point. As we look backward in time, the distance of Polaris from the north polar point was greater. At A.D. 1200, Polaris was 5° away from the pole; at A.D. 900 it was 6.7° away, and at A.D. 0, it was nearly 14° from the pole (Figure 7).

The Anasazi organized their buildings and living spaces on a north-south line without the assistance of a bright North Star. Other methods, more sophisticated than simply taking a sight upon a star would have been needed. Observing the position of sunrise and sunset on a given day would not have worked unless the horizon was perfectly flat.

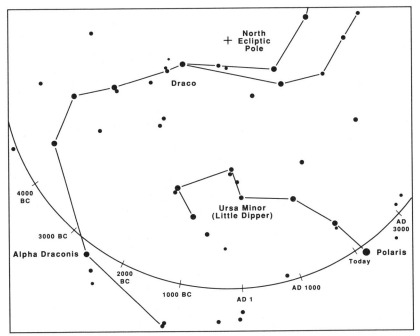

**Figure 7.** Movement of the celestial pole due to precession.

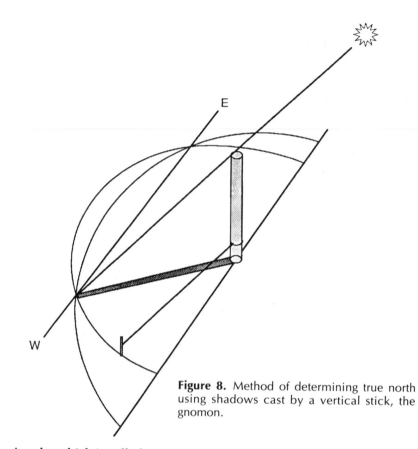

**Figure 8.** Method of determining true north using shadows cast by a vertical stick, the gnomon.

A pole, which is called a gnomon, may have been placed vertically in the ground by the Anasazi astronomer-priest and may have been used to determine geographic north. The gnomon, defined as a vertical, shadow-throwing pole, was used by many cultures—Borneo tribesmen, Babylonians, Greeks, and Chinese—to establish the length of the year and the time of the solstice by measuring the length of the shadow. The Kogi, living in the foothills of the Colombian Andes, establish temples with doors opening east and west using the gnomon. Likewise the architects of the great temples of India used shadows cast by upright posts to orient their structures to the cardinal directions.

The gnomon may have been used by the Anasazi in the following manner (Figure 8). Throughout the day the end points of the pole's shadow could have been marked by small stones or sticks. A rope attached to the pole could have been used to mark out a circle which cuts across the stones. A line drawn to connect the two places cut by the circle would run east-west; the line perpendicular to that direction would be north-south. If all these steps were performed carefully, and the stick had been aligned accurately to the vertical, the method should have allowed the Anasazi to align their structures with the kind of accuracy we have discovered amongst their ruins.

## The Celestial Equator

Like the earth, the sky has an equator, the celestial equator, which is the outward projection of the earth's equator. From the earth's equator, the celestial equator is directly overhead. Any object which lies on the celestial equator rises precisely in the east and sets precisely in the west. At the time of equinox the sun is on the celestial equator and spends 12 hours above the horizon.

On the earth we determine how far north or south of the equator we are by latitude: northern or positive latitude for the northern hemisphere and southern or negative latitude for the southern hemisphere. The distance which the sun, a planet, or a star is from the celestial equator is known as its declination, an exact counterpart to latitude on the earth. At the times of equinoxes, March 21 and September 21, the sun is exactly on the celestial equator, and its declination is 0°. At the time of summer solstice in the northern hemisphere, the sun is farthest above the celestial equator and has a declination of +23.5°; at winter solstice, its declination is -23.5° (Figure 9).

## The Path of the Sun

While the motions of the stars as they rise in the east and set in the west are very regular, the sun, the moon, and the planets wander across the celestial sphere in less regular patterns. Throughout the year the

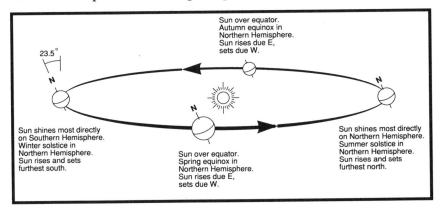

**Figure 9.** The seasons of the earth.

sun moves from west to east along its own particular pathway known as the ecliptic. The ecliptic is tilted by 23.5° from the celestial equator, and the sun takes one year, 365.24 days, for a complete circuit of the ecliptic.

Relative to the background stars, the sun moves about 1° per day, which amounts to twice its diameter per day. As a consequence, constellations shift their locations compared to the sun throughout the year. Each night a given star rises a few minutes earlier; at sunset, new constellations appear on the eastern horizon and move up higher and higher each night.

## The Rhythmic Sun

At the times of fall and spring equinoxes, September 21 and March 21, the sun spends equal amounts of time above and below the horizon. On those two days it moves across the sky on the celestial equator, rising in the east and setting in the west. Only if the horizon is perfectly flat will the rising and setting positions be exactly east and west. On the two days of equinox, the sky is divided into four parts: east and west, which are approximately established by sunrise and sunset; north and south, established when the sun is highest in the sky. Such a division of the dome of the sky into the four quarters clearly had great symbolic significance for ancient sky watchers as judged by the number of peoples who aligned themselves and their buildings along the four cardinal directions. Many cultures, such as the ancient culture of India described in the Vedas, considered March 21 to be the start of the new year. Equinox was the time for the Vedic priest to rebuild a ceremonial altar made of 360 bricks, in order to rejuvenate the old, exhausted year.

During the spring the sun rises each day farther north along the horizon and at noon reaches higher in the sky. Once the extreme has been reached, at the time of summer solstice, the sun pauses at its most northerly rising position for several days and then begins its downward motion toward winter solstice. As the days grow shorter, the sun's declination decreases until December 21.

This oscillation of the sun between summer and winter sunrise points along the horizon gave ancient astronomers a convenient calendar (Figure 10). For those who could read it, the horizon was a reliable time piece. If the horizon was distant and contained sharp peaks and clefts, the day of the year could be accurately determined at sunrise or sunset.

The cyclic motion of the sun is variable and repetitive: fast at equinox and slow at solstice. Reflected in the seasons—with the changes in

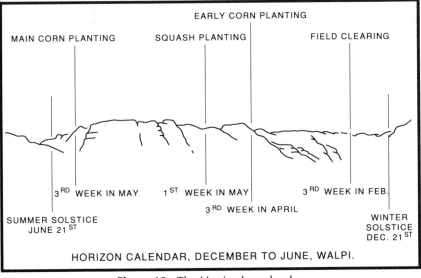

EARLY CORN PLANTING

MAIN CORN PLANTING          SQUASH PLANTING          FIELD CLEARING

3^RD WEEK IN MAY          1^ST WEEK IN MAY          3^RD WEEK IN FEB.

3^RD WEEK IN APRIL

SUMMER SOLSTICE
JUNE 21^ST

WINTER
SOLSTICE
DEC. 21^ST

HORIZON CALENDAR, DECEMBER TO JUNE, WALPI.

**Figure 10.** The Hopi solar calendar.

rainfall, duration of the day, temperature, and growing season—the sunrise positions were intimately linked with human life and the environment. How could they be ignored?

The sun does not move at a uniform rate along the horizon but noticeably slows when it approaches solstice, like a pendulum slowing at the end of its swing.  At the latitude of Yellow Jacket, at the time of equinox, the sun moves a full solar diameter, half of a degree, between successive days. Near solstice the sun's motion drops to zero, returning to practically the same sunrise point each day for a week. Solstice means "stand still" in Latin.

There was a potential danger in the stopping of the sun at the two end points of its swing along the horizon.  At the time of winter solstice, among the historic Pueblos there was concern that the sun would cease its motion forever, or even worse, that the sun might fall off the edge of the world.  The land might sink into a cold of unending winter.  Festivals were organized to send the sun on its way.[7]  At summer solstice, there was concern that the sun would pause too long at its summer house, throwing off the proper cycle of the year, shortening the agricultural year, and permitting a freeze before the time of harvest.[8]

## The Rhythmic Moon

During a month the rising moon swings between two extremes on the eastern horizon, similar to the oscillation of the rising sun during one year. The orbit of the moon is tilted with respect to the earth's orbit by 5°9'; perturbations cause it to vary from 4°57' to 5°20'. As a result, the moon can rise farther to the north of sunrise on summer solstice. While today the sun reaches a maximum declination of 23°26', the moon can reach a declination of 28°46'. When the moon reaches its maximum northern or southern declination, it has a "standstill" similar

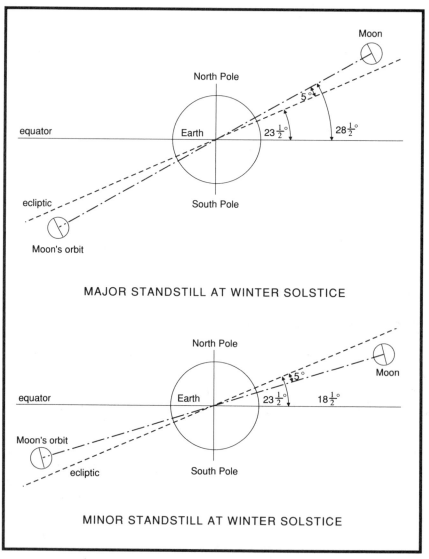

Figure 11. Major and minor standstills of the moon.

to that of the sun near solstice.  Due to the gravitational effect of the sun, the moon's orbit precesses with a period of 18.61 years. The major standstill is followed by the minor standstill 9.3 years later, when the moon swings in one month between declinations of ±18°7' (Figure 11). Major standstills of the moon were apparently detected by prehistoric inhabitants of northern Europe, as indicated at Stonehenge, other megalithic observatories,[9] and the recumbent stone circles of Scotland. The Anasazi may also have paid attention to the lunar standstills, judging from evidence at Chaco Canyon and Chimney Rock.

## Sun Time and Clock Time

The earth moves on an elliptical, not a circular orbit, around the sun. As a result, the speed of the earth in its orbit is not constant.  Moving faster when it is closer to the sun, the earth rhythmically speeds up and slows down as it swings around the sun.  Since we are living on an earth that is changing its speed constantly, it appears to us that the motions of the outside world speed up and slow down at various times throughout the year.

At the time of winter in the northern hemisphere, the earth is closest to the sun and is moving fastest.  The sun moves fastest along the path of the ecliptic near the time of the winter solstice and slowest at summer solstice.  It is not an obvious difference, but it is one which is noticeable if the days are counted.  In the northern hemisphere the winter half of the year is approximately eight days shorter than the southern half.

Because of this variation in the speed of the earth and the apparent speed of the sun in the sky, the time determined by a sundial usually differs from that of a wrist watch, which runs at a constant rate.  The wrist watch runs on a fictitious sun, called the mean sun.  When the mean sun is due south and highest in the sky, it is called noon, local mean time.

Ancient people would have had a sense of the cyclic nature of the seasons, and they probably would have experienced time as a variable feature of their lives. We have made time uniform and rigid through our technology of the clock, preferring the convenience of gears and crystals to the varying shadows of the sundial.  As we shall see, the Anasazi constructed their own unique versions of sundials, using the varying play of light and shadow upon stone to establish and celebrate the changing position of the sun on the dome of the sky.

• Monticello

Abajo Mts.

Dolores River

Edge-of-the-Cedars ▲

LOWRY ▲ ▲

YELLOW JACKET ▲

HOVENWEEP ▲▲

Comb ▲

Ridge

Mesa Verde ▲

Durango •

CHIMNEY ROCK ▲

UTAH | COLO

ARIZ. | N. MEX.

▲ UTE T.P.

▲

▲ AZTEC

• Shiprock

Farmington

SALMON ▲

San Juan River

Mummy Cave

Antelope Hse ▲

White Hse ▲

Chuska Mts.

Canyon de Chelly

▲

CHACO ▲▲

PUEBLO BONITO

▲ CANYON ▲

▲

PUEBLO PINTADO

▲ KIN YA'A

GUADELUPE ▲

CASAMERO ▲

Mt. Taylor

• Gallup

VILLAGE OF GREAT KIVAS ▲

Zuni △

• Grants

Laguna △

▲ PUERCO

Acoma △

| Anasazi Sites ▲ | Modern Pueblos △ |

# Three

## Sky Watchers

For clues to the riddles of Anasazi astronomy, we turn to today's Pueblo Indians. Pueblo culture has the reputation of being highly conservative, so it is reasonable to assume that many native traditions may have been carried on since Anasazi times. On the other hand, the historical Pueblos are descended from a mix of prehistoric southwestern people and doubtless have absorbed traditions from all of them. They have also experienced pressures, usually less than friendly, from nomadic Navajo, Catholicizing Spaniards, and land-hungry Anglos that have resulted in cultural adaptations that the Anasazi could not have imagined.

Some of the differences between the Anasazi and the modern Pueblos are obvious. Great kivas have disappeared from Pueblo architecture, while the elaborate masonry of the Anasazi has been largely supplanted by adobe bricks. The roadways and other features indicative of a centralized Anasazi authority have also disappeared. Whatever traditions the modern Pueblos may have retained of their ancient ancestors, the culture responsible for the Mesa Verde cliff dwellings, the Hovenweep towers, and the Chaco Phenomenon has been transmuted into that rich mixture of past and present which is today's Pueblo societies.

Today, no two Pueblos are alike, and no single voice can speak for the past. Pueblo peoples speak variations of four distinct languages, while the largest linguistic group, Tanoan, has three subgroups. Western Pueblos, such as the Hopi and Zuni, tend to be organized by kinship groups, while eastern ones, such as the Tewa, are dual in structure, with "Winter" and "Summer" people alternately dominating religious affairs. Western Pueblos emphasize solstice celebrations more than eastern ones. And while some groups have circular kivas similar to those dominant among the Anasazi, others have rectangular ones. Still others have none at all.

The upshot of all this is that while the nature of modern Pueblo society can provide insights into the lives of the Anasazi, analogies between historical and prehistoric practices should be drawn only with the utmost care (see Appendix). For example, anthropological reports indicating that Hopi, Zuni, and Keresan priests used light and shadow effects to date solstices increase the likelihood that such effects at Anasazi sites were intended for similar purposes. Observations that contemporary Pueblo peoples do not notice lunar standstills or record unique astronomical phenomena can weaken theories about the use of the Chacoan "sun dagger" or the supernova content of the Penasco Blanco painting. However, as many Anasazi traditions may have been lost or changed over the centuries, such observations do not definitively rule out the possibility of such ancient practices.

## Sunwatching

Sunwatching is one of the few traditions that can safely be termed pan-Pueblo.[1] Historical Pueblo Indians have watched the movements of the sun along the horizon, have observed the play of light through windows and portholes at crucial times of the year, and have established sun shrines at key locations. While observation stations are usually located in or near pueblos and are often unmarked, shrines are less accessible and frequently resemble cairns or other man-made structures. A religious official is generally responsible for making the anticipatory and confirmatory observations for important dates. Zuni used to have a special Priest of the Sun, called the *pekwin*, but when the last one died, his duties were assumed by the Rain Priest. At the Hopi villages, the head of the society responsible for the upcoming ceremony makes the solar observations necessary to determine the ritual's date. At the eastern pueblos, the Winter and Summer chiefs watch the sun during their respective periods of office. Finally, the War Chief is responsible for sunwatching at a few Keresan pueblos.

Early anthropologist Frank Hamilton Cushing reported that the Zuni *pekwin* made a daily pilgrimage to a nearby Zuni ruin to watch the sunrise as the spring equinox approached. The *pekwin* sat in a ruined tower near a pillar bearing the sun, moon, and star markings similar to those near Penasco Blanco, and a companion kept a count of the days remaining until equinox by notching a stick. Other methods of anticipating a crucial date by counting the days from a sunrise over a special feature of the horizon have included untying knots in a string and marking beams or wall plaster. The Zuni priest confirmed the equinox by noting when the shadows of what Cushing called "the solar monolith," the nearby Thunder Mountain, and "the pillar of the

gardens of Zuni" were aligned. Meanwhile, Cushing reported residents of Zuni were checking up on the Priest's accuracy by observing
the play of light along plates imbedded in the walls of their homes. A
window or porthole similar to those at Hovenweep Castle or possibly
at Pueblo Bonito allowed the rising sun to illuminate a certain spot
only on the crucial dates.[2] Some of the Hopi villages have used similar
devices for predicting dates.

More commonly, sunwatchers have simply observed the sun's
movement along the horizon at either sunset or sunrise from any convenient spot. At one Rio Grande pueblo, the area in front of the
Catholic church was a sun station; at Hopi, the roofs of clan buildings
often serve.[3] Knowledge of where to stand is apparently the private
property of the observer and is not necessarily marked for posterity by
glyphs or architectural features. Similarly, the decision of when to begin the observations seems, at least at Hopi, to be up to the discretion
of the watcher. One sun watcher reported that he began his observations from the time when the sun set behind a motel on Second Mesa![4]

Sunrise is usually the crucial time of day for horizon observations
as well as light and shadow observations, but practice varies according to the pueblo. At the Hopi villages, the eastern horizon is generally watched for ceremonies falling after winter and up to and including
summer solstice. But for ceremonies falling after summer and including winter solstice, the Hopi watch the western horizon. Part of the
reason for this difference may be that the San Francisco Peaks to the
southwest of the Hopi villages provide a distinct horizon calendar.
Further, the Hopi kachinas, or masked deities impersonated by Hopi
men, arrive at the villages near the winter solstice and are said to re-
side in the San Francisco Peaks. The Zuni apparently watch the sun at
both sunrise and sunset, while the eastern Pueblos primarily watch at
sunrise, although some of the Tanoans watch at sunrise for one half of
the year and at sunset for the other. In addition to the sunwatching
stations, most Pueblos place shrines at key points along the horizon.[5]
Cushing considered the tower at the Zuni ruin to be such a shrine, but
as it was located near a former pueblo, it was probably a typical sun
station. Shrines are often located out of sight from the pueblo and require some exertion on the part of the priest or initiate when he goes
to deposit prayer offerings at them. The western Pueblos seem to lo-
cate these sacred spots in the solstitial directions, although any site in
line with an important horizon marker may qualify for a shrine. At
Hopi and Zuni, the solstitial directions are seen as the cardinal ones,
while the equinoctial directions are more important along the Rio
Grande.[6]

## Moonwatching

Among all of the Pueblos, the moon figures importantly in both cosmology and mythology.[7] Cloaked variously in male and female personae, Moon is an intermediary between Sun and Earth, able to exert a favorable influence on the giver of life.[8] Thus, the historical Pueblos have been glad to see the moon in the daytime sky, while eclipses, when the moon would hide his or her face from the people, were frightening experiences. The historical Pueblos evidently have been unable to predict such terrible occurrences.[9] Whether it is viewed as a male or female entity, the moon is generally associated with fertility in humans, animals, and plants. Much of the puebloan moon lore revolves around women and children, and pregnant women are most vulnerable to the dangers of an eclipse. Near winter solstice at Zuni, prayer sticks, or symbolic offerings, are planted in the fields for both Sun and Moon, with women directing their offerings at the guardian of the night sky.

As the Penasco Blanco painting, located near a probable sunwatching station, suggests, the conjunction of Sun and Moon has been ritually important for Pueblo peoples. At Zuni, the *pekwin's* job was greatly complicated by the necessity of holding the winter solstice ceremony when the moon was full. The Zuni felt it important that the moon at its strongest should buttress the sun at its weakest; during summer solstice, the opposite held true, and the "strong" sun complemented a "weak" crescent moon. This emphasis on balance often meant that the dates for the solstitial celebrations did not correspond exactly to the actual solstices. Similarly, the important solstice-related celebration of Shalako was ultimately dated by solar observation, but preliminary rituals were performed according to the phases of the moon for nearly two months beforehand.[10] Among the Hopi, each important annual ritual, although timed by the sun, was assigned a specific month. Months bore names indicative of the rituals, activities, or natural phenomena unique to them.[11]

Eastern Pueblos watched the moon carefully for weather omens, with variously shaded rings corresponding to different gradations of cold weather. Like the Zuni, the Tewa, a Tanoan subgroup, have noted that the moon's path is similar to that of the sun, but it is only during full phases that it is seen to mimic the sun precisely. Seasonal names dominate for eastern Pueblo months, where appellations incorporating agricultural elements or weather patterns are common. Among the Zuni and the Hopi, the lunar element of timekeeping is more prevalent, but this is probably because these pueblos were spared the overwhelming contact with the Spaniards that the Rio Grande groups experienced. The Hopi may once have even timed certain rituals by a lunar horizon calendar.[12]

Although accounts are varied, most Pueblos seem originally to have recognized thirteen months as comprising a year. More manageable than the seasons and more practical than the days, the months were convenient timekeeping units. All pueblos seem to have conceived of the first visible crescent as the beginning of a particular moon, while the days of the invisible new moon were left uncounted. The problem of reconciling the lunar year with the solar was usually resolved by leaving one or two months unnamed and simply ignoring one of these if a discrepancy arose. Sometimes an additional "short" month would be incorporated to resolve the difference.

The Hopi and the Zuni had five and six named months respectively, followed by five or six more bearing the same names as the first series. For the Hopi, this practice represented the duality that underlay the structure of the universe. While the winter fields lay fallow, residents of the underworld were said to be cultivating and harvesting crops. The harvest obtained in the underworld, good or bad, would be duplicated in this world during the fall months. Similarly, while the Hopi were celebrating the summer solstice with a relatively meager ceremony, the elaborate winter solstice rituals were underway in the underworld, and while *Soyal*, the Hopi winter solstice festival, was in full swing, denizens of the underworld were holding the celebration of summer. Thus, the upper and lower worlds were mirror images of each other.[13]

## Star Gazing

Evidence of prehistoric Pueblo star watching is scanty at best, although many rock art panels do have stellar themes. Unlike sunwatching, star gazing does not require that the observer stand in a certain place, nor is the precision of light and shadow techniques necessary for the use of a star calendar. Among contemporary Pueblos, however, evidence for an avid interest in the night sky abounds.[14] Like those of many peoples, the cosmology of the Pueblos is headed by a supreme Sky God, who is omnipotent and all-encompassing. It was he, or he/she, as the deity is sometimes perceived, who initiated creation. But this god has retreated to the farthest reaches of the heavens, become abstract and inaccessible. The lesser gods, such as the sun, continue the work of the creator, interacting with humans and fueling the mechanisms of life.

Nevertheless, the great or morning star was sometimes seen by the historical Pueblos as representing the Sky God. Once, there may have been an earthly representative of this god, responsible for observing the movements of the morning star, much as the representatives of the sun make solar observations, while the heads of religious societies observe the moon and constellations. The morning star, together with its evening counterpart, also often represents the pan-Pueblo War Twins. These Twins were sons of the sun, and their exploits resulted in the establishment of many of the rules by which humans still live. Thus, the great star was the patron of warriors and of hunters; today, Pueblo peoples send it prayers for the fertility of their farm animals. Finally, the morning star, in conjunction with a crescent moon, has appeared on the masks of important Hopi kachina dancers, symbolizing the solstice.

The Rio Grande Pueblos watched the paths of the Great Bear, Orion, and the Pleiades, relying on the regularity of their movements for ordering their nocturnal rituals. In some cases, these rituals were timed by the passage of these constellations over the kiva hatchways. Tewa religious officials anxiously watched for the rising of Orion's belt near both solstices, believing that an early May appearance would mean a long growing season. Seen as a bridge between this world and the celestial realm, the Milky Way remains important to all of the Pueblo peoples and may once have been viewed as a god in its own right. Possibly, it, too, was once a metaphor for the omnipresent Sky God.[15]

While the traditions of the Pueblo peoples may have changed since Anasazi times, one important element in their lifeway has remained constant. The Pueblos are still agricultural peoples, needing a reliable calendar. They still live in a marginal climate, in a harsh environment that needs to be monitored constantly. Sustained drought and killing frosts are as serious for the Pueblos today as they were for the Anasazi nearly a thousand years ago. These kinds of concerns, more than anything else, link the modern Pueblos with their ancestors. The eyes of both peoples were fastened on the heavens.

# Four

## Chaco Canyon
## and Hovenweep

### Chaco Canyon

At first introduction, the land around Chaco Canyon, in northwestern New Mexico, seems as barren a wilderness as any on this planet. It may take several dramatic sunsets or sunrises, many days immersed in subtly shifting hues in sky, sand, and sage, before the casual traveler begins to realize that this empty desert is a land of power and beauty. Yet, for nearly as long as humans have walked upon the North American continent, some have chosen this lonely canyon for their home.

The San Juan River Basin has never been completely tamed. Even in today's world of automobiles, grocery stores, and other conveniences, this desert has resisted encroachment and discouraged settlement. But once, nearly a thousand years ago, a people turned what is now the middle of nowhere into the "Center of the World." They guided scarce rainwater to their crops and made the earth yield them food. Out of desert stone, they built tall, walled cities with towers, in circles and squares.

It was among the colorful sandstone cliffs of the canyon carved by the intermittent waters of the Chaco Wash that these ancient peoples constructed their religious and political center.[1] The settlements are crumbled now, and centuries of rain and snow have erased the whitewash from their walls, but the graceful, curved buildings on the canyon floor still tantalize the imagination. Some of the buildings recall the architecture of the Aztecs of ancient Mexico; others are reminiscent of styles used by other Anasazi groups to the north, such as the vanished inhabitants of the Mesa Verde cliffs. Still others are unique to Chaco.

The Chacoan Anasazi were not confined to the sacred space delineated by the canyon's variegated walls. Throughout northwestern

New Mexico, people subscribing to the cultural norms radiating from the canyon built towns, tilled fields, and set up shop. Scaling the Chaco cliffs by means of carved staircases, Anasazi messengers could travel along the nearly four hundred miles of roadways that linked the canyon settlements with the outlying ones.[2] Averaging 30 feet wide and often edged with low walls, these roads ran in remarkably straight lines radiating outward from Chaco Canyon all directions, attesting both to the engineering skill and the grandiose self-image of the society that built them (Figure 1).  As the Anasazi never invented the wheel and had no beasts of burden, the purpose of these roads remains enmeshed in the many mysteries of the Chaco Phenomenon.  One thing is certain: in the San Juan Basin of nearly a thousand years ago, all roads led to Chaco Canyon.

Chacoan communities were linked by more than roads. Bonfires may have flared from ingeniously situated towers and shrines, all-night reminders to important towns and villages of their ties to the Center.  While religious ceremonies were being held, these fires may have been especially important.  Whatever the reasons for the elaborate buildings, the intricate webbing of roads, and the signal shrines, they could only have been constructed by a highly organized and integrated society.

Of all the mysteries the Anasazi left behind, one question looms larger than all the rest.  We have ample evidence of the craftmanship of the ancient Chacoans, but what of their philosophy?  Were they simply pragmatic builders and businessmen who took these professions beyond all previous frontiers in the Southwest, or did these people possess a science, a coherent means of linking themselves with the cosmos?  What would the world look like through the eyes of a living Chacoan?  In short, how much did they know, and how did they apply what they knew?

One thing that we do know about the Anasazi is that what went on in the sky was of extreme importance to them, and they watched the heavens closely.  From the sky came rainwater and sunlight, both essential to survival in an agricultural society. Chacoans needed to know when to plant and harvest crops, when to prepare the irrigation systems for the onslaught of the summer rains, when to steel themselves for the winter months.  They also apparently needed to know how to orient their important buildings according to the cardinal directions, so as not to live against the grain of the cosmos.  These needs, together with the sheer pageantry of sunrise and sunset in the desert, could have made sunwatching one of the central activities of the priestly Anasazi astronomers.

The height of the Chacoan culture lasted from A.D. 1055 to 1083, cor-

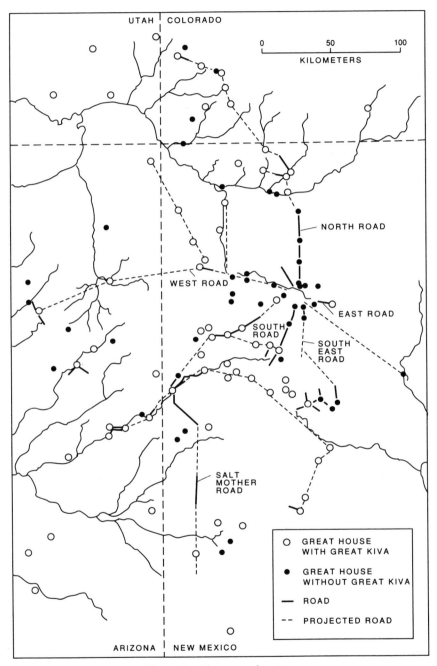

**Figure 1.** Chaco road system.

responding to the period of most intense building activity. This period also produced the most startling series of events in the heavens that have taken place within the last few thousand years. In July 1054 the supernova which produced the Crab Nebula blazed in the daytime skies for three weeks and remained visible at night for nearly two years. Some twelve years later, in 1066, Halley's Comet appeared, frightening Europeans on the eve of the Battle of Hastings. Another decade later, on March 7, 1076, a total solar eclipse was visible south of Chaco Canyon. In 1077 sunspots large enough to be seen with the naked eye were reported in China, beginning a more than two-hundred-year period of unusual sunspot activity. And again on July 11, 1097, another total eclipse passed over the Southwest. The inhabitants of Chaco Canyon may have been so startled and puzzled by these events that they became devoted sky watchers, investing much more effort in astronomy than they might have had the heavens been ordinary and unchanging.

The practicality of observing the sun's annual celestial journey, so crucial to survival in the marginal desert climate, was undoubtedly inseparable from the religious significance of those observations. In a desert world where life must be coaxed out of the environment, the sun's "decision" to return from its winter home, as well as its actual arrival at the northern extreme of its journey, is an occasion for celebration and thanksgiving.

To help identify the crucial times of year, the Anasazi of Chaco Canyon apparently practiced horizon astronomy. They may also have used the play of light and shadow on walls and rocks to confirm the dates suggested by the sun's position along the horizon. Solar observation stations have been found at sites ranging the entire length of Chaco Canyon. Theories about the extent of Anasazi astronomical knowledge and the uses to which they may have put these sites are controversial, but it is at least clear that the vanished sunwatchers knew when the solstices and equinoxes occurred. To date, five potential solar observatories have been identified in Chaco Canyon.

## Fajada Butte

One of the more recently identified and controversial of the solar sites at Chaco Canyon is atop a lonely butte that strikes the imagination with its stark isolation (Figure 2a).[3] Situated at the fork in the canyon near its eastern end, Fajada Butte dominates the vistas from most of the Chacoan great houses, and its top provides a view over long-dead cities. By remarkable good fortune, the artist Anna Sofaer was recording a spiral petroglyph near the butte's summit for a rock art survey

**Figure 2a.** Fajada Butte.

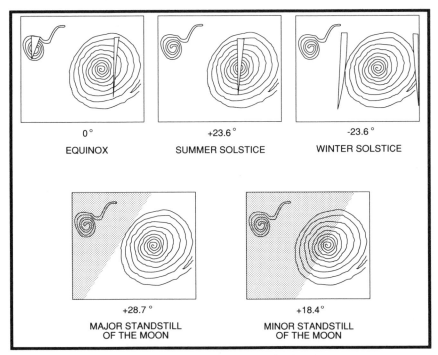

**Figure 2b.** Solar and lunar events at the three slab site.

one June day in 1977. Near midday, she observed that a dagger of light sliced through the spiral, located on a rock wall behind three slabs that apparently have fallen into place as a result of erosion. The "sun dagger" marks the equinoxes and both solstices and perhaps also the major and minor standstills of the moon (Figure 2b).

Because of the presence of "Mesa Verde" sites on Fajada Butte, the dating of the three slab site is uncertain; it has not been firmly established that the sun dagger site was contemporary with the construction of the Great Houses and with the culture identified as the Chaco Phenomenon.

The site consists of two spirals carved into the rock behind the three horizontal sandstone slabs. Just before noon on the days surrounding summer solstice, the knife of light bisects the larger spiral. At winter solstice, two noonday daggers frame the large spiral. Finally, during the equinoxes, the smaller spiral is bisected at midday by a lesser dagger, while a larger shaft of light passes to the right of the center of the greater spiral.

The large spiral has 19 grooves, which may reflect Anasazi knowledge of the 19.00-year Metonic cycle of the moon, the time required for the same phase of the moon to recur on the same day of the year. The slightly shorter lunar cycle of 18.61 years corresponds to the time between successive major standstills. At Fajada Butte the moon's shadow bisects the spiral at moonrise during minor northern standstill and just touches the petroglyph's left edge during major northern standstill. At both places a straight groove has been cut, which is parallel to the moon's shadow. Since the groove is tilted at the same angle as the moon's shadow, which is different from the angle of the sun dagger, it seems clear that Anasazi astronomers were aware of the major and minor standstills of the moon. Knowledge of the 18.6-year cycle or the 19.00-year cycle is remarkable for a culture that did not maintain written records. As we shall suggest in the next chapter, attention to lunar standstills at Fajada Butte may have been inspired by moonrises and winter solstice festivals at Chimney Rock Pueblo.

By the middle of May, an agricultural society would want to have planted most of its seeds, so as to take full advantage of the short summer growing season. Today's Hopi Indians, among others, do much of their planting at this time. In mid-May when the sun has a declination of 18.5 degrees, a shadow bisects the spiral at sunrise, and the observation of this event may have aided the Anasazi in determining when to plant their crops.[4] The position of the shadow is identical to that produced by the moon at minor standstill, and both functions may have been of importance.

The drama of the "sun dagger" could have been a commemoration of the regularity and predictability of nature. It may have been experienced as a time when the realm of the sacred intruded upon the plane of everyday life, as the living shaft of light moved across the immobile face of the rock. Probably the site was used to celebrate events that had been predicted by horizon watching: the dagger was an affirmation that all was well with the universe. Because of its location at some distance from any of the major towns of Chaco Canyon, and because of the difficulty of ascending Fajada Butte, the sun dagger is more like the shrines than the calendrical devices of the modern Pueblos. Aids for determining solstices, equinoxes, and planting dates are usually constructed in or near the populated areas, where they can be conveniently monitored. Shrines, however, are generally located at some distance from towns and villages and are often less accessible than calendrical sunwatching stations.

Today it is not sun priests who comprise the select few allowed to visit the Fajada Butte shrine. But rather they are anthropologists, astronomers, and other scientists studying the site who make regular pilgrimages. Because of the publicity about the "sun dagger," the numbers of tourists attempting to climb Fajada Butte began to threaten the fragile site. Access to the butte's summit is now by Park Service authority only.

## Wijiji

At the eastern extreme of settlement in Chaco Canyon stands the ruined specter of what may have been the last of the great towns to be built in the canyon. Here, at the very edge of the "world's center," the Anasazi may have watched the sun rise and set at winter solstice, the harbinger of snow and harsh winds, with fervent prayers for its northward return. A little beyond the ruins that are now called Wijiji, a staircase leads to a ledge along the canyon rim.[5] A faded sun symbol, probably painted by Navajo Indians, marks the site. Farther along the ledge are some boulders, one of which is marked with crosses and spirals, perhaps cut by the Anasazi. From just a few meters beyond this spot, a sun priest could have observed the winter solstice sun rising from directly behind a natural rock pillar on the other side of a bend in the canyon rim. And at sunset on the same day, the sun sets into a natural cleft in the rock ledge a short distance away.[6]

## Pueblo Bonito

The "Beautiful Town" that is Pueblo Bonito is the largest and one of the most impressive of the Chacoan ruins. Evidence of Anasazi famil-

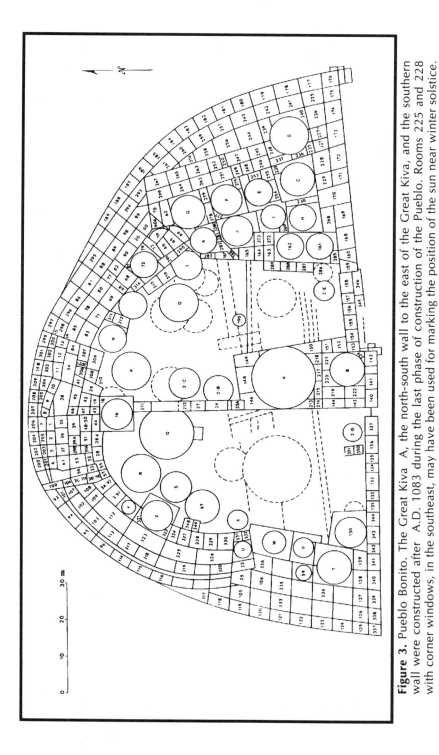

**Figure 3.** Pueblo Bonito. The Great Kiva A, the north-south wall to the east of the Great Kiva, and the southern wall were constructed after A.D. 1083 during the last phase of construction of the Pueblo. Rooms 225 and 228 with corner windows, in the southeast, may have been used for marking the position of the sun near winter solstice.

iarity with astronomical principles is enmeshed in the building's architecture. The wall that divides the building into eastern and western halves is oriented within 15' of true north. The western half of the south wall is oriented within 8' of true east. The great kiva in the eastern half of the Pueblo has a north-south axis with an orientation of 45' east of true north. These structures were built during the last major building stage in Pueblo Bonito between A.D. 1083 and 1123 (Figure 3).

Pueblo Bonito's walls are perforated with a number of "corner windows" or doorways that do not often appear in prehistoric Pueblo architecture. Two of these windows face east and provide good views of the winter solstice sunrise.[7] From these corner openings, a sun priest could have observed the sun's movement along the eastern horizon until the end of October. At this time, the sun begins to move along a portion of the horizon that is flat as viewed from the window. Just when this lack of distinguishing features makes the sun's movement difficult to discern, a narrow shaft of light strikes a wall opposite the window at sunrise. As winter solstice approaches, the beam widens and travels northward along the wall. At the solstice, the sunbeam neatly throws a square patch of light into the corner of the room.

Because the movement of the beam along the wall is so obvious from day to day, the corner window at Pueblo Bonito could have been used to predict the solstice as well as to confirm it. The Bonitan sun priests may have marked the plaster along the wall to keep track of the number of days remaining until the sun arrived at its winter "house." Anticipating important dates may actually have been the most crucial of the sun priest's duties; elaborate ceremonies in honor of the sun would take several days, even weeks, of preparation. Unfortunately, we can not be absolutely confident that the corner openings in Pueblo Bonito were intentional Anasazi sun stations because of uncertainties about the building's reconstruction. Outside walls may originally have blocked the views of the horizon and prevented the sunlight from entering the rooms.

## Casa Rinconada

On the south side of Chaco Wash, almost directly across from Pueblo Bonito, lies the great subterranean kiva that is Casa Rinconada. With a diameter of over 63 feet, this is one of the largest kivas ever built by the Anasazi, and it shares the architectural features of the great plaza kivas of the great houses across the wash. Unlike most of those kivas, Casa Rinconada stands alone, physically unconnected with any village or town, although its location suggests an association with the small "village" sites that dot the canyon's southern half. It is not clear whether Casa Rinconada served as a communal religious structure linking the villages or was a meeting place for people who lived on both sides of Chaco Wash.

Whomever it served, Casa Rinconada was constructed with great attention to detail, and, as we have already noted, it may have been a symbolic representation of the Anasazi cosmos. One axis of symmetry was established by the line connecting the north and south doorways; the axis is within $1/3°$ of true north. Twenty-eight niches ring the kiva's walls; the line from the eighth to the twenty-second niche was also very closely aligned with true east-west, within 8' of arc. A twenty-ninth niche may have been lost in the reconstruction. These niches may have been related to the 29.5-day lunar months. The remarkable accuracy of alignment of this large and complex structure to the true cardinal directions was demonstrated by Ray Williamson.[8] The care with which Casa Rinconada and portions of Pueblo Bonito have been built in parallelism with the larger cosmos is a powerful insight into the symbolic world of the Anasazi.

The sockets for the four roof supports form a square, each side within $1/2°$ of the cardinal directions; the western and eastern pairs have orientations of 0°29' and 359°24' respectively. These posts may also have symbolized the directions of the sunrise and sunset at summer and winter solstices, an orientation system that prevails in Zuni and Hopi pueblos.

In addition to the 28 niches, there are six larger and less regularly spaced wall crypts. During the summer solstice sunrise, a beam of light enters a northeastern opening in the kiva and settles into niche E (Figure 4), an effect first noted by Williamson.

It is, however, problematic that this effect was planned by the Anasazi. At one time, a room was constructed outside the crucial opening in Casa Rinconada, but it is not known if the room existed throughout the kiva's use. In any case, the original size of the opening is unknown. Furthermore, if the northeastern post that supported the kiva's roof was 16 inches in diameter or larger, the sunbeam would have been blocked. Sixteen inches is not an unreasonable diameter for a roof support for a kiva of Casa Rinconada's size; one of the supports of the great kiva at Chetro Ketl measured over 26 inches. And finally, there is some evidence that a screen of mud and wattle was mounted along the wall in front of the niches, preventing sunlight from touching the niche or its contents.

## Penasco Blanco

Not far from Penasco Blanco, a great house located atop the cliffs at the western extreme of the canyon, park surveyors discovered an un-

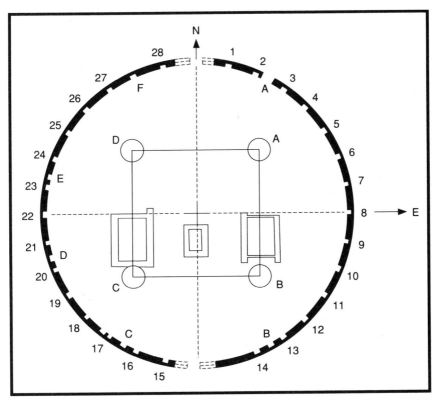

**Figure 4.** Casa Rinconada. The alignments of the roof supports are: C–D, 0°29′; B–A, 359°24′; D–A, 90°33′; C–B, 89°35′. Niche E is illuminated by sunlight at summer solstice dawn.

usual Anasazi rock painting. With red paint on the underside of a low overhang, a Chacoan artist depicted a sun, a crescent moon, and a star, signing his work with the hand print that marks a site as sacred in the Pueblo tradition (Figure 4). Anthropologist Frank Hamilton Cushing, who lived with the Zuni Indians for nearly five years in the late 1800s, described an almost identical set of symbols painted on a pillar marking a Zuni sunwatching station.[9] Although the view to the east from beneath the Penasco Blanco pictograph is not conducive to sun-watching, the eastern horizon as viewed from the cliff top directly above the site does contain the distinguishing features needed for a good horizon calendar.[10]

A lively debate has revolved around the depicted conjunction of the crescent moon with the large star. While the morning star and crescent moon combination is a favored motif in Pueblo mythology and art, it is also possible that the Penasco Blanco painting represents the A.D. 1054

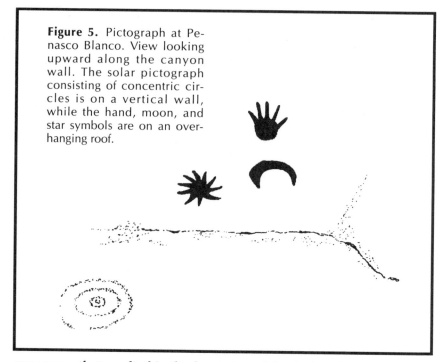

**Figure 5.** Pictograph at Penasco Blanco. View looking upward along the canyon wall. The solar pictograph consisting of concentric circles is on a vertical wall, while the hand, moon, and star symbols are on an overhanging roof.

supernova that resulted in the formation of the Crab Nebula.[11] That supernova would have been visible in the American Southwest at the beginning of Chaco Canyon's peak period as a cultural center. The exploding star, which would have shone brightly enough to be visible during the day, would have appeared in conjunction with a waning crescent moon. While historical Pueblo peoples have no distinct tradition of recording unusual astronomical phenomena for posterity, there have hardly been enough supernovae for us to determine whether such a dramatic event would indeed have been excluded from public recognition.

Surely a Penasco Blancan observed the supernova, and possibly he painted it. Unfortunately, we have no clear means of ascertaining the probability that a prehistoric Pueblo Indian would have depicted a unique astronomical event like a supernova. But while we cannot know whether a long-dead priest painted a dying daylight star, we can be certain that he intently watched a living one.

## Hovenweep National Monument

The land near Hovenweep National Monument, in southeastern Utah, seems even more harsh than that surrounding Chaco. Even the

Navajo, who chose the adjacent areas for their homeland, call this spot the "Desolate Place." Built above a small spring at the head of a box canyon, the main ruin at Hovenweep hints at a desperate existence. Most of the important dwellings are perched in easily defensible positions along the rims of the box canyon, as though guarding the precious source of water. The inhabitants apparently opted against vulnerable windows, relying on small "portholes" to provide minimal light and ventilation. (Many of the small holes present in the ruins today were originally used as sockets for cross-braces for the high, thin wall.) Free-standing towers, both round and square, rise throughout the settlement and are especially prominent near the spring, the entrances to the canyon settlements, and the storage crypts.

Whatever threats they may have faced, if indeed they faced any other than the harshness of the environment, the Anasazi of Hovenweep built their astronomical perceptions into their villages.[12] The well-preserved walls stand tall against the glaring desert sky even today, hinting at secrets within. And secrets abound. Hovenweep is the site of some of the best documented and least controversial Anasazi light and shadow calendars.

## Hovenweep Castle

Named for its resemblance to the fortresses that dotted the European landscape during the Middle Ages, Hovenweep Castle stands on the rim of the main canyon, above a cool spring. The D-shaped tower to which a number of rooms were attached is actually just a small part of the entire building as it once appeared. A terraced pueblo, now collapsed, may once have risen from near the canyon floor to adjoin the structure, then much taller, on the rim. A rectangular room, dubbed the "sun room," was attached to the southern side of the tower, and it is this room's ground floor to which archaeoastronomers have been drawn (Figure 6).

From this room, the Anasazi of Hovenweep Castle could mark the equinoxes and both solstices and could have obtained an indication of an early spring planting date as well. At the summer solstice sunset, a ray of light streams through a porthole in the sun room, shining on the lintel of the doorway into an eastern room (Figure 7). At winter solstice sunset, a porthole on another wall lets light fall on the lintel of the passage to the tower. These effects, first discovered by Ray Williamson and co-workers,[13] together with the alignments of Casa Rinconada and Pueblo Bonito, were the first unambiguous indications of the careful attention to astronomical detail by the Anasazi.

In all of these cases, the play of light along the wall is noticeable well before the actual date of the solstice or equinox, allowing Anasazi sun

**Figure 6.** Hovenweep Castle: beam of light from setting sun at summer solstice, 1986. The two photographs show the movement of the patch of light just before sunset. Just as the light fades it touches the edge of the doorway.

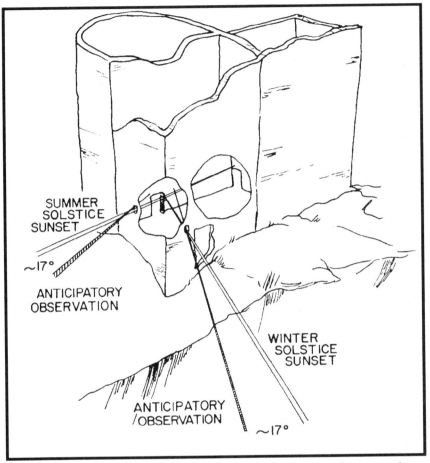

**Figure 7.** Diagram of Hovenweep Castle showing summer and winter solstice alignments. The possibility of anticipating the events is indicated. Note the similarity of the alignments of ports and doorways at winter and summer solstice.

priests sufficient time to plan the appropriate ceremonies. In early April, when the sunray is first visible inside the room, the Anasazi would have been preparing for the year's first planting. The long, north wall of the room, along which the beam travels as the solstice approaches, could well have been scored with vertical marks indicating the planting dates for various crops.

## Unit-Type House

Perched on a boulder only a few hundred yards east of Hovenweep Castle, Unit-Type House consists of six rooms and a kiva and probably

housed only one or two families. Four portholes perforate the intact
wall of the eastern room. Light from the rising winter solstice sun enters one of these ports and falls in the room's northwest corner near a
protruding wall. At summer solstice, another port allows a shaft of
light to fall into the room's southwestern corner. This effect occurs
nearly an hour after sunrise, as a giant boulder prevents rays from the
rising sun from reaching the port. At the equinoxes, an area of the
wall halfway between the low extending wall and the southwestern
corner is illuminated at sunrise. Cushing reported that ordinary Zuni
families kept tabs on the accuracy of the sun priest's predictions by
means of portholes in the walls of their homes.[14] Perhaps the solar
events commemorated at Unit-Type House were engineered by such a
family, to ensure that the sun priest got it right.


## Cajon Group

About six miles southwest of the Hovenweep Castle and its surrounding settlement, again tightly surrounding a spring, lies the
ruined Cajon Group. The western wall of a tower room there is
pierced by three portholes. Two admit the light of the setting solstitial
sun, while the other is oriented to the equinox sunsets. As there are no
special features or markings where the beams strike the inside wall, it
is impossible to confirm whether these ports were intentionally
devised as calendars. At winter solstice, rays from the setting sun
probably would have been blocked by a nearby building. But the
light's movement along the wall prior to and following the equinoxes
would allow both anticipation of the events and, in the spring, the determination of planting dates.

The tower building may have an additional calendrical function in
relation to another building a short distance to the west.[15] Shortly after
fall equinox, the western building casts a shadow over part of the tower
building, with the shadow moving northward until it covers only the
western wall of the tower at winter solstice sunset. The shadow then
reverses its path until the spring equinox, when both buildings are un-
shadowed. Shortly afterward, the tower building begins to cast a shadow over its western counterpart at sunrise. The shadow effect appears
to continue on the western building until some time near summer solstice, but the ruined state of the tower building prevents determination
of the exact date. While it cannot be known if the Anasazi deliberately
constructed the two buildings to serve as a giant seasonal sundial, they
would have at least taken note of the coincidence of the shadowing effects with the seasons and made use of that coincidence.

**Figure 8.** Sun dagger near Holly House, Hovenweep. As the sun rises the single shaft of light coming from the left, near the spiral, is joined by a second shaft emerging from the right.

## Holly House

Near Holly House, located in one of the smaller canyons at Hovenweep, two huge boulders stand near the canyon wall. The two, with an overhang on one creating a roof, form a tunnel that opens to the east. A third boulder blocks most of the tunnel's western egress. The Anasazi carved two large spirals and a sun symbol similar to the one in the Penasco Blanco painting into the side of the southern rock. The sun first enters this natural corridor in late February, when preparatory work in the fields would begin and when some modern Pueblos start their seedlings in the heated atmosphere of the kivas. At spring equinox, it briefly illuminates only the sun symbol. After the equinox, the sun withdraws from the corridor entirely, reappearing in mid-April to light the concentric sun circle again. The rising sun continues to illuminate this symbol until May 20, when the Anasazi would want to have finished all but the final planting of their crops. Again the sun withdraws from the tunnel, only to make a dramatic return near the summer solstice. At that time, Williamson discovered that the rising sun throws two narrow beams of light onto the spirals and the sun symbol. The lines of light stretch out toward each other from these carvings, meeting at the center of the blank wall between them (Figure 8).[16]

As probably was the case at Fajada Butte, the Anasazi did not move the huge boulders into place to achieve the required play of light along the carvings. Rather, they must have noticed the unique patterns formed by the rising sun at summer solstice and carved the designs accordingly. The solar display at Holly House may have been used as a calendar for much of the planting season, as well as for confirmation and celebration of the summer solstice.

The solar sites at Hovenweep, like those at Chaco Canyon, testify to Anasazi ingenuity both in utilizing natural phenomena, such as the moving shafts of light at Fajada Butte and near Holly House, and in engineering novel effects of light and shadow, like those at Hovenweep Castle. As the solar portholes in the residential Unit-Type House indicate, astronomy was apparently important to all members of Anasazi society.

# Five

## Moonrise and Sunrise Over Chimney Rock

Nearly a hundred miles north of Chaco Canyon, the double spires of Chimney Rock dominate a collection of over a hundred sites, some of which may have served as Anasazi versions of astronomical observatories. The area contains evidence of eight semi-independent communities of late Pueblo I and Pueblo II age (A.D. 925-1125).[1] The chimneys and the associated high mesa have been recognized by the Taos Pueblo of northern New Mexico to be a shrine dedicated to the Twin War Gods of Pueblo mythology.[2]

The most dramatic and in some ways the most mysterious ruin of the area is that of the isolated Chimney Rock Pueblo set on the high mesa just below the pinnacles, 1200 feet above the water and agricultural lands of the valley floor (Figure 1). The pueblo, which has been identified as a Chacoan outlier,[3] contains two kivas and 35 ground floor rooms; a second story may have added an additional 20 rooms to the structure. The core-and-veneer masonry of the town is similar in style to that of the great houses of Chaco Canyon.[4] The Chaco-style East Kiva contains a horizontal, sub-floor ventilator tunnel and vertical shaft and a five-foot-high banquette upon which were built eight beam rests. Other features characteristic of Chaco-style kivas are a western subfloor vault and no evidence of a sipapu. The East and West kivas were set within a quadrangle of walls, which had been filled by the prehistoric inhabitants to the level of the kiva roofs, forming courts within the building (Figure 2). Another similarity to Chacoan buildings is the L-shaped layout of the building, the two arms of which enclose the East Court.[5] A bench has been built along the east-facing exterior wall in the East Court, providing a place to view the double chimneys.

Among those sites identified as Chacoan outliers, the Chimney Rock Pueblo is distinguished by being the most isolated, the highest, and the most remote from arable land. With two exceptions, building at all of the outliers was begun between A.D. 1086 and the first half of A.D. 1120. Chimney Rock Pueblo is one of those exceptions, as construction began in A. D. 1076.

The excavations of the Chimney Rock Pueblo by Professor Frank Eddy of the University of Colorado revealed that the interior and exterior walls of the pueblo had been placed directly upon bare sandstone bedrock, indicating that prior to construction the upper mesa was a bare rock platform without soil or vegetation. Every piece of the tons of rock and adobe necessary for construction apparently had to be carried up to build the large structure. Since there is no water on the mesa, construction may have been carried out during the winter when snow could have been melted for mixing the adobe mud. But it is doubtful that snow could have provided all the water necessary. We

**Figure 1.** Chimney Rock Pueblo (5AA83) looking east at the time of excavation by the University of Colorado.

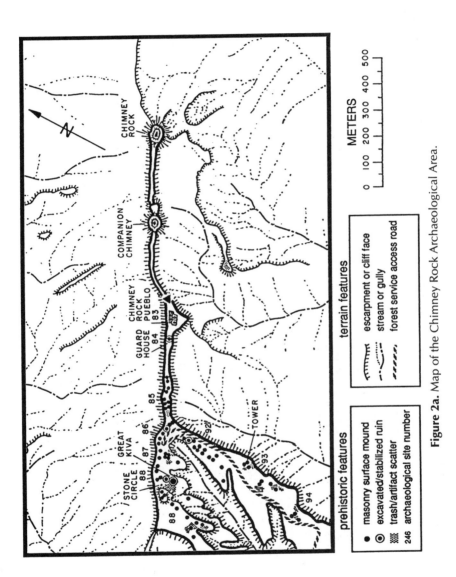

**Figure 2a.** Map of the Chimney Rock Archaeological Area.

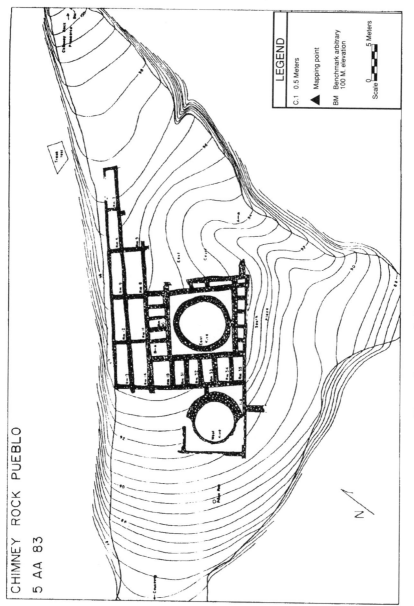

**Figure 2b.** Map of Chimney Rock Pueblo.

can imagine a steady stream of people working their way upward the thousand feet from the valley floor carrying pitch-coated wicker baskets filled with sloshing water.

Drainage of cold air into the floor of the valley may have resulted in a shorter growing season in the valley floor than on the upland terrain. Corn requires somewhat over 100 frost-free days to mature, and in order to achieve such a growing season, the Anasazi farmers in many areas were forced to move away from the most fertile agricultural lands closest to the Piedra River in order to get above the pool of cold air. However, those who were responsible for constructing the Chimney Rock Pueblo could not have been driven solely by a search for a longer growing season. The high mesa on which it is built is reached only by a narrow causeway of rock, falling off steeply on both sides. Passage to the mesa is blocked by an unusual structure known as the Guard House. The space beyond appears to have been set apart from ordinary activities. The overall sense of the Chimney Rock Pueblo is that it was not built for practical purposes but for its closeness to and commanding view of the double spires.

## Lunar Standstills

During May and June of 1988 our archaeoastronomy team surveyed portions of the Chimney Rock Archaeological Area for evidence of astronomical activities by its prehistoric inhabitants. Because of the connection between the Twin War Gods and Venus, we first looked for evidence that the planet may have risen between the Chimneys when the pueblo was occupied. Instead, we discovered that the moon would rise in the gap between the pinnacles, near the time of the major northern standstill. These predictions were confirmed on August 8, 1988, as shown in Figure 3 and on the cover photograph. For periods of little more than two years each 18.6-year period, the moon reaches a sufficiently high northern declination to rise between the pinnacles as seen by watchers near the Chimney Rock Pueblo. The sun never reaches far enough north.

The dates of the northern standstills in the latter half of the eleventh century were A.D. March 1057, October 1075, and June 1094. When we compared these with dates obtained by Eddy from logs found in the Chimney Rock Pueblo, we were astonished to discover that the two episodes of construction of the pueblo correspond with the last two lunar standstills of the century. Could the pueblo have been built primarily to observe the moon coming up between the chimneys? Could the spectacle of the moonrise have so captured the attention of not only priests from Chaco, but the local inhabitants, that it justified the immense effort required for construction on that remote mesa?

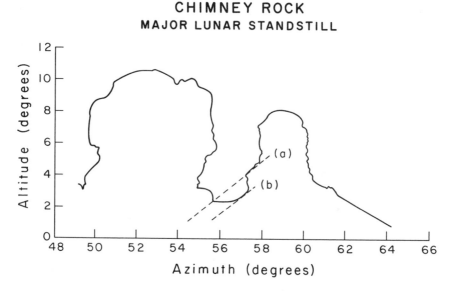

**CHIMNEY ROCK**
**MAJOR LUNAR STANDSTILL**

**Figure 3.** Chimney Rock as seen from a location northwest of 5AA83. The paths of the center of the moon at two declinations (a: 28.7°; b: 27.9°) are shown.

The tree ring dates suggest a connection.  A ponderosa pine pole taken from the lower and original horizontal ventilator of the East Kiva applies to the first episode of construction and gives a date of A. D. 1076. As seen from the Chimney Rock Pueblo, the first appearance of the moon between the chimneys during that standstill occurred in the fall of 1073. We estimate that it appeared between the chimneys on more than forty occasions through the fall of 1077.

The second set of dates from the East Kiva corresponds to the time the floor was filled and raised to establish a higher floor with a second horizontal ventilator shaft.  The East Kiva and adjacent Room 8 were roofed over with logs which were cut in the summer (June and July) of 1093.  The summer cutting of the logs is indicated by incomplete 1093 growth rings.  Trees were cut during the growing season, an unusual practice for an agricultural group, which usually engaged in winter, off-agricultural season cutting. The first moonrise of this standstill that occurred between the chimneys took place in the fall of 1092.

One interpretation of the agreement in the dates of construction  and the northern lunar standstills is that the Chimney Rock Pueblo was built primarily for astronomical observation and associated ceremony. In the East Court, in the courts above the kivas, and on roof tops, people could have gathered to observe moonrise through the foresight of the double spires.  It was not necessary for those responsible for planning and construction to have knowledge of the 18.61-year lunar cycle. Anticipatory observations of moonrise at the start of each northern standstill were clearly possible, and an accurate year count would have been unnecessary.

The most important astronomical event visible from the town may have been the spectacle of the full moon rising between the chimneys near the time of winter solstice. Among the historic Pueblos, sun and moon watching established the ceremonial calendars.[6] The various lunations throughout the year were given names and were associated with ceremonial activities. The Zunis attempted to organize their calendar so that winter solstice occurred at or near full moon. White Shell Woman (the moon) helps to persuade the sun to return north at winter solstice.[7] The coincidence of full moon and winter solstice would also have provided an important opportunity to bring the solar and lunar calendars into agreement. At Hopi the sun chief watched the setting sun to establish the date of *Soyal*, the winter solstice ceremony. In the *Powamu* ceremony, which followed *Soyal*, the *Powamu* Chief planted beans in a kiva at the time of the full moon.

In both of these pueblos, the rising full moon would have been carefully watched near winter solstice. The inhabitants of Chimney Rock Pueblo may have been similarly watchful of the rising moon. The full moon always rises at sunset. When it rose between the double spires above the snow covered landscape, colored red from the glow of sunset, the moon must have appeared huge and brilliant. The sight of the moon rising between the chimneys ranks as one of the great dramatic events of the heavens. Our Anasazi predecessors could not help but have been impressed.

Every 19.00 tropical years (the Metonic cycle in which a given phase of the moon will occur on the same date of the year) the full moon will rise close to the time of winter solstice. Because the period of regression of the lunar nodes is 18.61 years, every Metonic cycle will not yield a full moon near standstill. During Metonic cycles in the eleventh century, the moon reached its maximum northern declination close to winter solstice on 1055, 1076, and 1095.

We speculate that in 1057 residents of the Chimney Rock area discovered the full moon rising between the chimneys at winter solstice. That time was just a few years after the appearance of the Crab Nebula supernova, and unusual events in the sky may still have attracted great attention. Nineteen years later the full moon again rose between the chimneys at winter solstice. But before that event occurred, a solar eclipse took place on March 7, 1076. Trees were cut in the summer of 1076, and portions of the pueblo may have been completed in time for the winter solstice moonrise of December 13, 1076.

The pueblo was rebuilt in 1093, and again the full moon could be seen rising between the chimneys in winter solstice of 1095. Those who remained at the pueblo through the summer of 1097, perhaps a year after the moon had ceased rising between the chimneys, would have been treated to another total solar eclipse. On July 11, 1097, the line of totality passed over Chimney Rock, and the view of the eclipsed sun from the High Mesa would have been spectacular.

The priests of Chaco must have played pivotal roles in both construction and ceremony. There appears to have been a precise and detailed transference of masonry technique, architectural planning, and kiva construction between Chaco Canyon and the Chimney Rock Pueblo. Masons and architects are typically males in early societies. Since they seem to have had minute knowledge of ceremonial architecture, Eddy suggests that those responsible for constructing the pueblo were knowledgeable priests from Chaco.

The ceramics found at the Chimney Rock Pueblo have the same manufacturing and style traditions found throughout the Chimney Rock area, and it thus appears that Chacoan women did not accompany the masons, architects, and priests. The potter's craft is primarily a female-related industry in pre-wheel agricultural societies. Eddy proposes that in the latter part of the eleventh century, small groups of religious elites left Chaco Canyon, perhaps due to religious schisms which selectively affected the high-status priests. Arriving without women, the men married local women, who manufactured the pottery used in the pueblo.

An alternate interpretation is that the immigrant priests were not accompanied by the full range of Chacoan society because they did not come to settle in the Chimney Rock area. They may have traveled northward for the specific purpose of observing moonrise between the chimneys and celebrating the winter solstice from the high mesa. Pilgrimages along the great roads into Chaco Canyon to visit the great houses at time of festivals have been proposed. At the time of lunar standstills the Chimney Rock Pueblo may also have became a major pilgrimage center.

Knowledge of the lunar standstill cycle in Chacoan society is indicated by the three slab site on Fajada Butte[8], which was discussed in Chapter 4. There has been considerable doubt that the Anasazi of Chaco Canyon paid attention to lunar standstills.[9] Part of that skepticism was prompted by the lack of any other examples of lunar standstill observations in the Anasazi cultural area or in Mesoamerica. Now we have the additional example of Chimney Rock. Furthermore, the three slab site has been difficult to interpret because of the lack of any firm dates associated with the spiral petroglyphs. There was, in addition, the question of the ceremonial or practical relevance of standstill. The standstill of the sun was obviously important, but who would have cared about the standstill of the moon?

At Chimney Rock we encounter a visually dramatic situation which provides accuracy in both prediction and confirmation. The 19-year and 18.61-year cycles were intertwined and both may have been ceremonially important and calendrically relevant. The lunar standstill marking on Fajada Butte and the 19 turns on the spiral could have been inspired primarily by the Chimney Rock experience.

## Summer Solstice

At the time of summer solstice sunrise, many of the sites of the High Mesa Group are aligned with the higher chimney and the sun on the astronomical horizon. To walk along the upward sloping causeway toward the high mesa in the pre-dawn hours, watching the high chimney back lighted by the eastern glow, is an unforgettable experience. Prehistoric observers facing eastward at any of the the High Mesa sites would have seen the broad glow of summer solstice dawn behind the chimney and may have identified that spire and/or that location as the northern home of the sun.

How would Anasazi observers have determined the dates of summer solstice? As seen from the Chimney Rock Pueblo, the sunrise on the distant horizon is blocked by the high chimney for at least a month prior to solstice. Similarly, the other sites along the top of the mesa have their views of the horizon blocked by the chimneys and the higher portions of the mesa. Where could a horizon calendar been observed? There is a one tower on the high mesa, located above the south-eastern cliffs. Observations of the rising sun throughout the year could have been easily made from the top of the tower. Anasazi towers are puzzling structures, for their functions are unclear: defensive, ceremonial, communication, living, storage, or astronomical uses? In this  case, the tower may have been constructed as an observing platform for the sun watcher.

At the western end of the High Mesa, 164 feet from the Great Kiva, is a partially dismantled stone circle containing a circular basin, 14 inches in diameter, cut into the bedrock. These stone circles and their associated basins appear to be primarily a Chacoan phenomenon.[10] The stone circle and basin at Chimney Rock reaffirm the Chaco connection and may have marked a ceremonial location for viewing the high chimney back-lighted by the sun at summer solstice dawn.

## Equinox Sunrise

If the double pinnacles were used as such an important foresight for the rising moon, we would expect they would have been used elsewhere in the area for the rising sun. During the summer of 1988 we framed this as a hypothesis that we could test. Elsewhere there must be other sites using the chimneys as foresights for the sun.

As seen from the high mesa, the sun never rises far enough north to fit between the pinnacles, but to the west, across the valley on a ridge above the Piedra River, the sun at equinox rises between them. On the ridge there are 12 sites[11], each of which would have provided a view of sunrise between the chimneys at some time of the year. The largest site in the group, 5AA8, the probable political and ceremonial center of that community, contains three kivas and a two-story room block. We visited the ridge at the fall 1988 equinox and discovered that the site is located only 80 feet south of the east-west line passing through the center of the gap. As seen from 5AA8, the lowest portion of the gap, 2.2 miles to the east, has an azimuth of 89.6° (Figure 4). Since the ridge offers many equally suitable locations for habitation, it seems likely that this particular location was chosen because of its alignment relative to the chimneys.

Because the gap between the chimneys has an elevation of 3.5° as seen from 5AA8, the sun will not rise between the chimneys on the

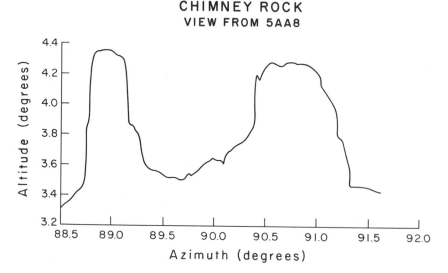

**Figure 4.** Chimney Rock as seen from the ridge west of the Piedra River at the ceremonial site, 5AA8.

morning of equinox, but will appear between the pinnacles on the morning of March 25. That date is close to half of the day count between summer and winter equinox (March 24). In a mountainous environment such as Chimney Rock, the location of an observing site due east of the elevated chimneys would not have been an easy task; several stations at which gnomons were erected may have been necessary. An east-west alignment would have been easier to establish than the date of equinox.

Similarities of architectural styles suggest close ties between the communities east and west of the Piedra River. If 5AA8, which does not appear to be Chacoan in architectural style, was an observing site similar to the Chimney Rock Pueblo, both the native Chimney Rock population as well as the intrusive Chaco colony may have been involved in astronomical ceremony and calendrical observation. Which came first? Perhaps the Chacoans learned of the dramatic astronomical phenomena associated with the solstices and came northward to construct their structure on the highest mesa below the chimneys. The first occupation of some sites of the High Mesa Group predate the construction of the Chaco outlier by more than a hundred years. Prehistoric inhabitants of the area may have been observing moonrise and equinoctial sunrise between the rock spires as early as the 8th or 9th century.

# Six

# The Yellow Jacket Ruin

Montezuma Basin is a tranquil, dramatic, and fertile land. The soil is plowed into rolling red swells. Pinto beans, wheat, and alfalfa provide striking contrasts of green upon furrowed red. In the quiet light of late afternoon when the furrows are darkened by long parallel shadows, it is a place of unforgettable beauty. The plowed fields surround scattered Anasazi ruins, small broken castles of rocks overgrown by tall stands of sage. Above and beyond the fields to the east rise the mountains of the La Platas. To the south is the rounded mass of Sleeping Ute Mountain. At night the stars shine in the clear air as brightly as at any mountain observatory and continue undimmed down to the dark mountains of the east and south. The rainfall of 16 inches per year is twice that of either Hovenweep or Chaco Canyon, and it is easy to understand why the Anasazi would have chosen such a place as this in which to live.

In the Montezuma Basin a peak Anasazi population of 30,000 may have been distributed among eight major settlements, each of which may have functioned as ceremonial centers for surrounding villages and hamlets. In order of size, these eight centers were Yellow Jacket, Lowry, Sand Canyon, Goodman Point, Mud Springs, Yucca House, Lancaster Ruin, and Wilson Ruin (Figure 1).[1] Yellow Jacket has evidence of at least 120 kivas, while Lowry, Sand Canyon, and Goodwin Point contained approximately 110, 90, and 85 kivas respectively.

Although the northern Anasazi never reached the stage of building cities, the larger settlements, especially that of Yellow Jacket, may be viewed as incipient cosmic cities. With slightly larger populations and perhaps a more complex social structure, some of these larger Anasazi settlements may have joined the ranks of classic ancient cities such as those of Mesoamerica: Teotihuacán, Copan, Palenque, and Tenochtitlán. Each of these major ancient cities in Mesoamerica was designed to be cosmic in scope, the mythical center and birth place of the universe.[2] For those who lived in its vicinity, Yellow Jacket too may have been the center of the universe.

**Figure 1a.**

**Figure 1b.**

**Figure 1.** Artist's conception of two of the ceremonial centers of Montezuma Basin. (a) Yellow Jacket and (b) Goodman Point. North is on top. Yellow Jacket contains at least 120 kiva depressions while Goodman Point contains approximately 85. Great kivas are respectively in the north and southwest of Yellow Jacket and Goodman Point. Both sites have rows of kivas approximately aligned east-west. Goodman Point has both north-south and east-west walls; Yellow Jacket has a north-south road extending southward from the Great Kiva. The standing monolith is at the southern edge of Yellow Jacket.

The cosmic cities of Mesoamerica appear to have functioned as market places, fortresses, and administrative centers as well as sites for ritual and ceremony. They were nourished both by pilgrims and by the inflow and outflow of foodstuffs and goods. As a result, they acquired great economic and political power.

Ceremonial centers were self-amplifying. They stimulated population increases, and their populations were organized in the construction of monumental structures, such as the pyramids of the Maya, the palaces of China, and the temples of India. The development of a high level of agricultural technology was clearly necessary. The leaders must have had considerable administrative sophistication as food surpluses had to be collected, stored, and redistributed; irrigation systems had to be designed and repaired; and agricultural land needed to be developed and maintained.

The organization of the ceremonial centers appears to have been inspired by a way of thinking that has been called "cosmo-magical," in which builders perceived a relationship between the celestial order above them and the biological rhythms of life. The two realms were seen as parallel in structure and synchronized in time. The cosmic city was aligned with the cosmos. Its streets and structures were often carefully oriented to the cardinal directions. The pattern of life within the city in its festivals and celebrations resonated with the movements of sun, moon, planets, and stars. The goal, either intuitively felt or officially imposed was a synchronization of individual human life with the larger universe. Such a goal, that of harmony between the individual and the larger cosmos, is evident in the lives of the Pueblo people as well as in the structures built by their ancestors.

## Yellow Jacket

Situated at an elevation of 6800 feet, the Yellow Jacket ruin lies on a nearly flat mesa above Yellow Jacket Creek, with a sharp, serrated, eastern horizon suitable for sunwatching. The site, close to water and good farmland, is convenient for living and superb for astronomical observation.

Yellow Jacket was one of the first of the northern Anasazi ruins to be explored, having been visited by the geologist J.S. Newberry in 1859. The ruin is located near one of the major springs of the high plains between the Abajos of Utah and the San Juan mountains of Colorado. The spring was a watering place and stop for stages in the past century.

The first detailed survey of the site, designated 5MT-5, was made by Professor Joe Ben Wheat of the University of Colorado.[3] Professor Wheat has been the major figure associated with the archaeology of Yellow Jacket since 1954 when he began to excavate sites in the area. His first excavations were of a Basketmaker pithouse of the Stevenson Site, 5MT-1. Following that, he has led continuous and extensive excavations yielding a uniquely comprehensive picture of the area. He considers the large ruin to be the major unexcavated Anasazi site in the Southwest and believes it to have functioned primarily as a ceremonial center.

## A Walking Tour

Unlike the ruins of Chaco Canyon, Mesa Verde, or Hovenweep, Yellow Jacket lies entirely upon private land. Permission to enter the site must be obtained from the owners, the Archaeological Conservancy and the Arthur Wilson family, and is granted normally only to those who have a research program involving the ruins.

Yellow Jacket may represent the highest single concentration of kivas of any Anasazi site in the Southwest (Figure 2). Most of the kivas

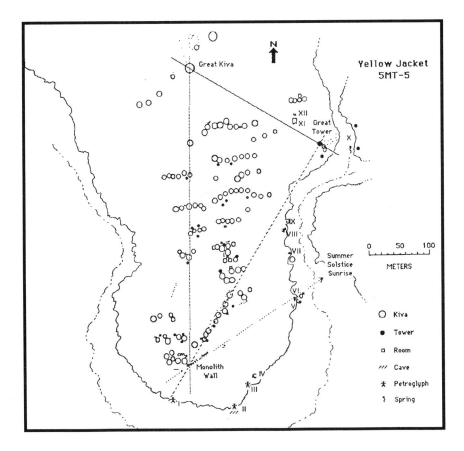

**Figure 2.** Map of Yellow Jacket. The locations of twelve suspected shrines are indicated.

are organized in rows aligned east-west, visible today only as shallow saucer-like depressions, 15 to 25 feet in diameter, covered with thick, deep sage. Typically, north of each kiva depression there are remnants of a block of rooms running parallel to the line of kivas. Next in abundance to the kivas and associated room blocks are towers, over 20 of them distributed among the kivas. In the northern and the southern edges of the ruin there are two large mounds, apparently the remains of three story buildings.

We invite the reader to an imaginary guided tour of this ruin, not as fulfilling an experience as climbing over rocks, but it has the advantages of avoiding the ear-loving gnats and the thick clumps of sage. As we drop down into the Yellow Jacket Canyon to approach the ruin from the south, we step centuries back in time and enter a world set apart. The plowed fields, farm houses, and grain elevators disappear from view, blocked by the enclosing walls of the canyon. The stream flows quietly among cattails and scrub oak. Small fish dart along the channel, startled by our shadows as we step over the rocks of the stream. The small tributary to Yellow Jacket Creek has a 10-foot waterfall, beneath which lies an inviting large pool of dark water.

Moving up the rocks toward the mesa, we encounter in its southernmost cliffs a small cave with several kiva depressions in front of it (Figure 3). The low cave, 10 feet deep and some 30 feet wide, is filled with fine, white ash. Joe Ben Wheat believes it to be the sacred remains of the the fires which once burned in the kivas of the mesa overhead. Over the cave, pecked on the rocks, is one of the three Yellow Jacket

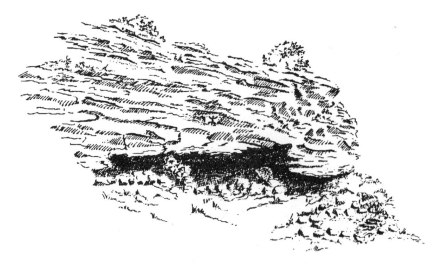

**Figure 3.** The Cave of Ashes.

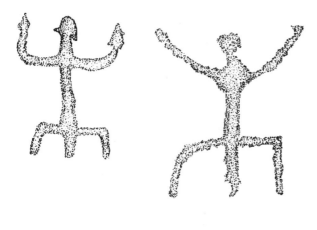

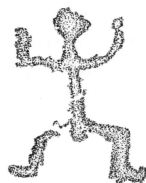

**Figure 4.** Petroglyphs of Yellow Jacket.

petroglyphs (Figure 4).  Its full meaning is forever lost to us, but the figure is perhaps representative of man, lizard, or horned toad. It and the two other nearly identical petroglyphs establish significant directions in space and important locations of the ruin.

We move a short distance westward along the base of the cliffs and reach an ancient trail winding to the top of the mesa. As we emerge above the cliffs, the world which we had left so recently reappears around us. To the northeast are the three great snow peaks, Mt. Wilson, Wilson Peak, and El Diente, all over 14,000 feet.  Directly east are the many summits of Mt. Hesperus and its companions, still mantled with snow in early June.  But our attention is drawn forward to the wall of ruins some 150 feet away spread across the northern horizon. The line of rubble contains room blocks, walls, kivas, and towers, culminating in the east in the high southern mound.

Rabbits scamper through the sage, and turquoise lizards sun themselves; there is even an occasional rattler. As we start working our way through the tall sagebrush, we create great yellow clouds of pollen. Ahead, we can not help but notice the solar monolith, its flat face gleaming in the sun.

The sun appears to have been the major astronomical object that the Anasazi observed, and the standing stone, five feet high and shaped into a wedge at its top (Figure 5), is the most obvious evidence of solar ceremonialism on the site. Its wedge-top is aligned toward Wilson Peak near the location of sunrise on June 21. On the morning of summer solstice, the pointed shadow of its top falls across the ruined wall of the room just to the west of the monolith. Throughout the weeks before solstice the position of the sharp top of the shadow could have been marked on the wall and would have provided an accurate calendar.

To the west and east are four additional fallen monoliths of similar size (Figure 6). These monoliths and many smaller blocks define a wall directed toward the solstice sunrise point. The Anasazi spoke to no living informant nor left us any written description of what they considered sacred and important in their lives. But here in this line of stones is a dimly heard voice and a faintly seen astronomical ritual. The distant mountains and the rising sun were clearly very important to those who lived here.

Beyond the monolith wall there is one break in the rubble, a narrow passageway just north of the standing monolith. Continuing past the monolith, we enter the great basin, surrounded on three sides by rooms, kivas, and towers. On the western edge of the basin is a partly broken earthen dam, suggesting that during perhaps wetter times this great bowl functioned as a catchment basin. However, the inhabitants of this ruined city would not have needed a reservoir for farming as the agricultural lands were some distance to the north and west. Likewise they may not have needed the water for domestic purposes for the distances to Yellow Jacket Creek and its tributaries are short. Water is precious in this land, and the water held in the basin behind the dam may have been used primarily for ritual and ceremony.

We move northward past the great basin along what is now a well defined northern road, some 30 to 45 feet wide in places, passing between many pairs of kiva rows. Here we are in the heart of the ruin, in the kiva complex containing some 80 closely spaced, aligned kivas. After walking for more than a thousand feet north of the solar monolith we encounter the Great Kiva, a rounded crater 60 feet in diameter. The Great Kiva has been placed so carefully along the north-south line that it departs by only one-half of a degree from true north as seen from the solar monolith.

**Figure 5.** Standing monolith.

**Figure 6.** Eastern monolith.

Further to the north of the Great Kiva rises the northern mound, a portion of which has been unfortunately carted away for road fill some time in the past. Standing on its top and looking southward we begin to appreciate the size and complexity of this ruin. A short distance northward plowed fields begin. The regularity of the swells of the land hints at further kiva rows. How much farther north from us does the ruin extend? We may never know, for much has been lost under the farmers' plows.

## Solstice Sunrise

We were drawn to Yellow Jacket by the mystery of solstice sunrise, and in the coolness of dawn we rose on many mornings during our summer field work to watch the brightening sky above the eastern mountains. Each day before summer solstice the sun rose slightly northward of the previous morning. Its northward movement slowed noticeably as it approached the great massif of El Diente and the Wilson peaks. The rising sun climbed the southern side of the massif, and then one morning it stopped and paused. The mountain appears to act as a barrier to the northward moving sun. Did the sun seem to the ancient sun priest to be returning to his northern home after a year's journey (Figure 7)?

**Figure 7.** Sunrise at summer solstice at the standing monolith. The shadow of the monolith is cast upon a board placed at the location of a suspected wall.

For the Hopi, the sun may be an animate being who travels back and forth from south to north, from his southern house to his northern house. As seen from Yellow Jacket, such a northern house would have been the Wilson–El Diente massif; not merely an abstract point on the horizon, it may have been viewed as a real habitation in which the sun resided for some four days. Offerings are made by the Hopi when the sun is in his summer and winter houses, requesting his benevolence toward them and their crops.

Today, somewhat wiser by nearly a thousand years of astronomical observation and theory, we approach the dawn with a different set of preconceptions. The sun rises each morning because the earth turns on its axis and in that slow turning a hot ball of gas is carried into view. But it is easy to imagine an ancient sun watcher, standing at the edge of the mesa in the dim light, waiting for the first evidence of the sun in his summer house, enthralled by the beauty of the beginning of the day. Some 10 to 15 minutes before the appearance of the upper edge of the sun's disk, dark beams, known as crepuscular rays, often fan outward from the cleft in the eastern mountains between El Diente and Wilson Peak. It is in that place that the diffuse glow of the dawn first becomes concentrated. During the minutes remaining before sunrise, the sun creeps southward below the horizon, hidden behind the Wilson–El Diente massif. The sun's presence is revealed by the increasingly bright glow of dawn and by the crepuscular rays which rotate slowly counterclockwise while their focus moves south. First the sun is beneath the northern gap. Then it is hiding behind El Diente, and finally, just before its appearance above the horizon, it hides behind the long southern ridge of Mt. Wilson (Figure 8).

When the sun eventually appears above the southern ridge of El Diente, it is blinding, red, and gorgeous, but it is no surprise. Its rising point has been fully anticipated. That first hint of concentrated brightening is a magic time when the uncertainty of night is replaced by the certainty of the sun's location, when creation of the day seems assured. We can now only speculate about the complex meaning of those stones of the solstice line and the great effort which went into their careful placement. They speak to us of the sacredness and mystery of those eastern mountains and solstice sunrise.

## Anticipation of Summer Solstice

As seen from the ruin, there is a small horizon feature just to the south of Mt. Wilson with a flat top and straight sides looking similar to the rock monoliths themselves. The monolith-like feature, especially dramatic and prominent during the half hour just before sunrise, may

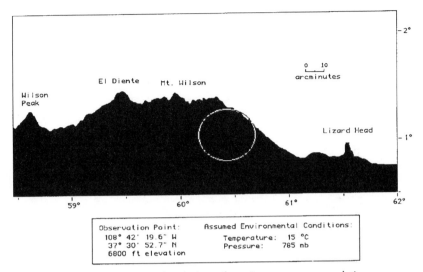

**Figure 8.** Computer simulation of sunrise on summer solstice.

be another example of anticipation in the life of the Anasazi. The horizon rock is Lizard Head Peak, 13,113′ in elevation, and on the morning of June 5 the sun rises behind it as seen from the southern portion of the ruin (Figure 9). This unusual event provides a precise and dramatic observation by which to anticipate the date of summer solstice.[4] After observing the first sunrise behind Lizard Head, the sun priest would know that some 16 days remained until the actual solstice. By notching a calendar stick or tying knots in a rope, he could accurately determine the number of days remaining as the sun continued to move farther north toward Mt. Wilson. Because the sun has no noticeable motion along the horizon at the time of solstice, accurate determination of solstice requires observations at earlier or later times. Furthermore, sufficient time for preparation for the ceremony was probably needed; dances had to be rehearsed, costumes made, and food prepared.

Whatever meaning the sunrise behind Lizard Head may have had for the Anasazi, it is, even today, a remarkable event. As the red sun is struggling to rise above the horizon, it appears to be stabbed by the rock peak. We wonder what stories may have grown up around that astronomical event. It is a long and perilous journey for the sun, a journey vitally necessary for the earth to break out of the winter's cold. As an animate being, the sun may have been subject to the vicissitudes and uncertainties of the natural world. Mesoamerican deities—Quetzalcoatl, for example—were often fragile beings who could suffer pain and defeat. Quetzalcoatl lived in uncertain relationships with the un-

**Figure 9.** Sunrise behind Lizard Head.

predictable natural world. In Mesoamerica as well as in a number of other cultures, the daily and annual cycles of the sun are depicted in terms of battles with the forces of darkness and disorder. The sun's encounter with Lizard Head, as seen from Yellow Jacket, may have been viewed in local myth as one of those challenges and tests which the sun had to undergo each year.

## Shrines

Located primarily along the eastern half of the perimeter of 5MT-5 are 12 places that may have been prehistoric shrines. In the most general sense, a shrine is a human-made structure or a natural feature that is held in sacred esteem. Pueblo shrines are often located on the tops of mesas, are typically to the east of habitation sites, are frequently stone enclosures, and may be associated with rock art. Pueblo shrines are often locations where offerings are placed and can be features such as caves, mountains, rock formations, springs, and pools.

The great Anasazi migration of A.D. 1300 resulted in the movement of people living north of the San Juan River into the Rio Grande valley and the Pajarito plateau of northern New Mexico. It is to this area and its ancient and modern inhabitants that we turn for clues about the meaning of shrines. A well-known living shrine on the Pajarito Plateau is that of the Stone Lions in Bandelier National Monument. Within a circular ring some 20 feet in diameter, enclosed by large slabs of volcanic tuff, lie two crouching lions facing southeast. Each lion is about six feet long, including two feet of tail. The shrine is now visited by Indians from several pueblos and is apparently dedicated to hunting. Visitors who walk from the Monument Headquarters in Frijoles

Canyon to the Stone Lions find broken pottery, shells, feathers, petrified wood, obsidian, many bleached antlers, skulls, and bones of deer and elk. The shrine is about a half a mile northwest from the ruins of the village of Yapashe, the traditional ancestral home of the Cochiti.

According to modern Pueblo traditions in the Rio Grande valley, shrines on high points protect the world.[5] They are especially powerful when they are placed on mountains at the four cardinal direction of space. Around the Pajarito Plateau there are stone enclosures which may have been shrines on high places and hilltops near almost every important ruin, most often to the east of each ruin.

Caves are important shrines for the modern Pueblos, who believe that they can come into close contact with the powers of the underworld when they store ritual implements and make offerings in caves.[6] Earth Mother remained underground after the first people emerged through the *sipapu*. Specific caves and small lakes are considered by various Pueblos as the *sipapu* opening. All springs are assumed to connect with the underground lake from which come the rain spirits. Offerings presented to Earth may be ears of corn with prayer feathers attached, feather bunches, prayer sticks, food images, or small pieces of food, and they may be placed in caves or substitute *sipapu* shrines such as circular stone enclosures.

The cult of caves is one of the most ancient of the pan-Mesoamerican world. Caves are frequent features of the Mesoamerican sacred landscape and are pictured extensively in rock paintings, murals, and codices going back to the time of the founding of Teotihuacán.[7] The family of symbols including caves, water, mountains, fertility, and maize form the nucleus of the Mesoamerican religion. The rain and mountain god, Tlaloc, corresponding to the Maya god, Chac, was one of main deities of ancient Teotihuacán. Together with the sun and war god, Huitzilopochtli, he presided over the fierce and bloody rituals performed on the Templo Mayor of Tenochtitlán.[8] These symbols of water and sun, placed upon the summit of the great pyramid-mountain of Templo Mayor, dominated the Aztec world.

Sacred springs and pools are also located at the cardinal points of several of the Rio Grande pueblos. Until 1902 the major ceremonialists of Acoma would make a semiannual trek with solar offerings to their *sipapu* lake or spring somewhere in the vicinity of Cortez.

The largest stone enclosure of the mesa top at the main Yellow Jacket ruin is a semicircular enclosure, to the south and east of the solar monolith (Figure 10). The enclosure is open precisely to the east, has a diameter of nearly 20 feet and is constructed out of large sandstone slabs averaging two feet in length. This structure is similar in size to the circle of stones surrounding the Shrine of the Stone Lions.

**Figure 10a.** Southeastern shrine, triangulation of stones.

**Figure 10b.** Drawing, southeastern shrine.

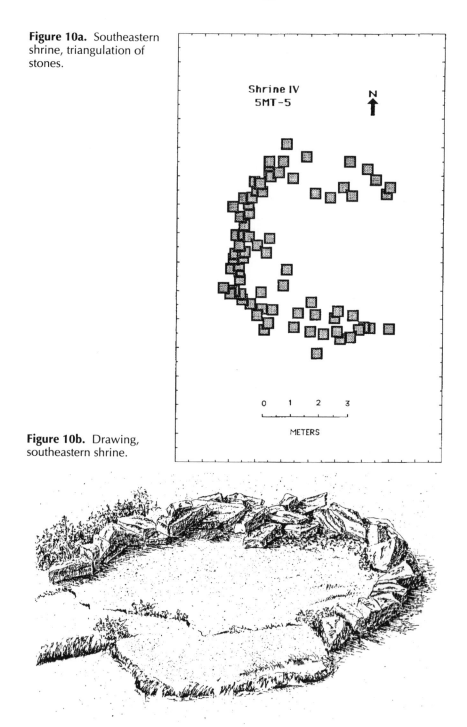

Shrine IV
5MT-5

N

0   1   2   3

METERS

A short distance to the north is a similar, but smaller enclosure, also open to the east. It is aligned with the monolith wall and has been placed just above the largest cave in the eastern cliffs. The enclosure is on the line between the standing monolith and the position of the rising sun. Its location is similar to that of a possible shrine near Shabik'eshchee in Chaco Canyon, which is located between a sun symbol and the position of sunrise on summer solstice.[9]

The location of this enclosure in the direction of summer solstice suggests that it functioned as a site for offerings to the sun. Immediately below is the large eastern cave, which, if dedicated to Mother Earth, would have provided a powerful conjunction of sun and earth symbolism. The eastern cave has an opening more than 60 feet across and is 12 feet tall at its highest. Numerous shaped stones across its front indicate that buildings had once been constructed within the cave. A tower, kiva, and small block of rooms are located on the slope below the cave. Further down the slope is a series of terraces, which because of their sheltered position may have been used for early planting of ceremonial crops.

## Great and Small Kivas

The three mapping projects at Yellow Jacket have identified slightly different numbers of kiva depressions. Wheat's map shows 129, while that of Ferguson and Rohn shows 147. Our mapping project in 1987-88 included only those kiva depressions for which we could identify a clearly defined center and rim. Generally when we surveyed a kiva depression with the theodolite, we measured five points on the rim and the center. Our work located the position of 117 kivas, of which 79 were contained in east-west kiva rows. North of the kiva rows are blocks of rooms and to the south are middens. Wheat believes that the majority of the kivas were constructed during Pueblo III times (A.D. 1100-1300) upon the remains of Pueblo II (A.D. 900-1100) *jacal* structures. He suggests that the character of the site evolved from primarily domestic to ceremonial, functioning during Pueblo III times as the ceremonial center with only few permanent inhabitants who were responsible for ritual activities.

The ceremonial heart of Yellow Jacket may have been the Great Kiva at the northern end of the north-south road. Totally unexcavated, it now is an impressive bowl some 69 feet in diameter, set in a forest of dense sage (Figure 11). The center of the Intermediate Kiva, 600 feet to the south, lies only slightly more than an inch off true south from the center of the Great Kiva. As seen from the center of the Intermediate Kiva, the center of the Great Kiva would have been slightly less than

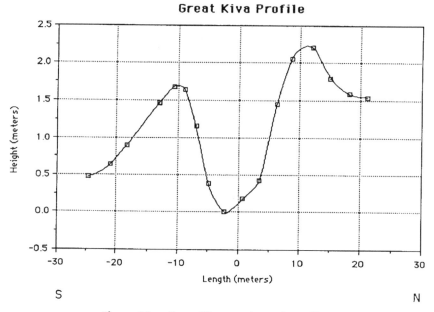

**Figure 11a.** Great Kiva, north-south profile.

one minute of arc away from true north. The smallest angle which the
unaided human eye can discern is approximately one minute. The
Great Kiva may have been linked to the Intermediate Kiva by a ceremonial pathway, which had been designed with an extraordinarily accurate alignment.

The Intermediate Kiva also lies due west of the Great Tower. From
the center of the Intermediate Kiva the Great Tower has an azimuth of
90° 58′. The line running due east from the center of the kiva crosses
the rim of the Great Tower. A sight line may have cut diagonally across
an opening in the Tower, in a manner similar to that of the Caracol of
Chichén Itzá.[10] An observer within the Great Tower, looking through
an opening in its walls may have been able to watch the sun at equinox
setting directly over the Intermediate Kiva or the sun at summer solstice setting over the Great Kiva.

## Lines to Ancient Skies

Many of the structures of 5MT-5 lie along three prominent lines each
of which points to a significant direction in the heavens. The three
groups served no obvious utilitarian or architectural purposes other
than delineation of space or astronomical symbolism and ceremony.

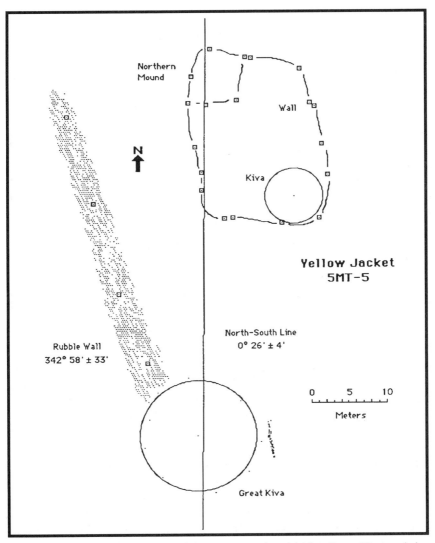

**Figure 11b.** North-south line is shown passing through the Great Kiva and the northern mound.

They radiate outward from the solar monolith with a spacing of approximately 30°.

The Great Kiva, the Intermediate Kiva, the northern mound, and the standing monolith are members of the north-south group which has an azimuth of only 26' east of true north and a length of over 1600 feet (Figure 12). This line departs from true north by less than the angular diameter of the sun. The accuracy of this alignment is comparable to

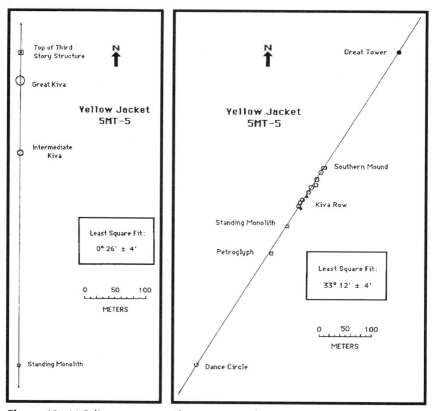

**Figure 12.** N-S linear group connecting the northern mound and the standing monolith.

**Figure 13.** 33° line connecting the Great Tower of 5MT-5 and the Dance Circle of 5MT-3 on the next mesa to the southwest.

that found at Casa Rinconada in Chaco Canyon. By comparison, the accuracy of placement of these structures still can not compete with that of the greatest monument of the ancient world, the pyramid of Kufu at Giza, erected about 2600 B.C. The worst alignment of its huge base, covering more than 13 acres, is on the east side. It departs from true north by a mere 5.5′

The Intermediate Kiva emerges as an important and unique structure, with the Great Kiva to the north, the Great Tower to the east, and the standing monolith to the south. Unlike most of the structures of 5MT-5 the Great Kiva, the Intermediate Kiva, and the Great Tower lack associated middens, indicating that they were never used for extensive habitation.

The road southward from the Great Kiva of 5MT-5 may have been the locus of a ceremonial journey similar to those which have been proposed for the road systems of Chaco Canyon. Celebrants may have left the Great Kiva, symbolic of the place of emergence, moved past the kiva rows and through the basin of sacred water, toward the symbol of death, the Cave of Ashes.

Slightly more than 30° from true north, the second line connects the Great Tower of 5MT-5 with the Dance Circle of 5MT-3 on the next mesa to the southwest over a distance of some 2500 feet (Figure 13). The line includes other important features, such as the the southern mound, a row of eight kivas (the longest kiva row on the site which is not aligned approximately east-west), two towers, the standing monolith, and the southwestern petroglyph. The perpendicular to the line lies within a few degrees of winter solstice sunrise.

The third line, that oriented with summer solstice sunrise, is rotated approximately 60° away from true north (Figure 14). Its length, from the fallen western monolith to the eastern stone enclosure at the edge of the cliffs, is nearly 760 feet. It too may have been a ceremonial pathway leading from the high point near the standing monolith to the possible shrine above the eastern cave.

The solstice group also serves as a symbolic boundary. Southeast of the solstice line the only structure on the mesa top is the large enclosure open to the morning sun. Symbols of darkness, birth, and water are present to the north of the line. To the southeast of the line, the sun and the symbols of fire and death dominate.

**Figure 14.** Group consisting of monoliths and possible shrine aligned toward the position of sunrise at summer solstice.

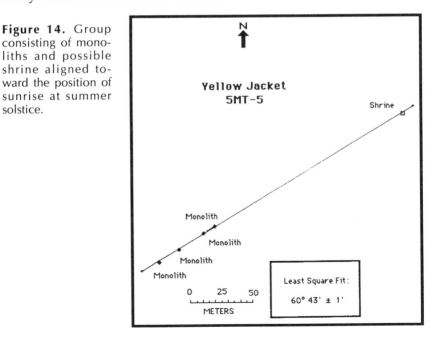

These three lines serve to join together important artificial and natural features of the landscape. Each starts in the north with major symbolic features: (1) the monumental structure of the Great Kiva, perhaps representing the origin of the world, (2) the northeastern Great Tower, and (3) the mountains, the eastern cave, and the solstice sun.

And there are more lines. A fourth line, only slightly deviating from true east proceeds from the southern mound to the eastern cave. The kiva rows and their middens also run east-west. The fifth line, from the Great Kiva to the Great Tower, leads toward the position of the sun at winter solstice. Each of these lines continues to be separated by approximately 30°. The sixth line, which should have an azimuth of 150° has not yet been found.

The importance of carefully defined linearity to the builders of 5MT-5 is strongly implied by the results of our surveys. Elsewhere in the Anasazi world, ceremonial linearity appears to be present in the extensive system of roads in Chaco Canyon. Long, low walls are also found in Chaco Canyon, some of which are associated with roads and others appear to separate and organize space.[11] The northern terminus of the North Road is perhaps symbolic of the origin of the world,[12] and passage along the road may have involved re-enactment of a creation mythology in which the first people emerged from the underworld and moved southwest to their present homes.[13]

While we do not wish to imply contact between these far-separated cultures, the linear groups of 5MT-5 are similar to the system of lines or *ceques* radiating outward from the center of Cuzco, Peru.[14] A series of shrines, or *huacas*, were also placed along lines which had astronomical significance, and these shrines were sequentially visited at specific times of the year. The 328 sacred *huacas* which were contained on the *ceques* appear to have been Peruvian counterparts of pueblo shrines and consisted of rocks, caves, hills, springs, houses, road junctions, and towers. Each *huaca* was worshiped on its particular day. About one-fourth of the *ceques* have identifiable astronomical alignments. The full system of *huacas* and *ceques* functioned as a complex calendar which integrated time, the surrounding topography, and social groups.

## Conclusions

Whatever the meaning of its architectural symbolism, the complexity of organization of 5MT-5 is an important revelation about the sophistication of Anasazi society. The obvious care with which the linear groups have been established, the intricate interrelationships of the groups, and the manner by which the groups integrate features of the natural environment indicate the importance of astronomical ceremony for the designers and inhabitants of Yellow Jacket.

What is the significance of this apparent fascination for astronomy amongst the Anasazi of Yellow Jacket, Hovenweep, Chimney Rock, and Chaco Canyon? Sunwatching was undoubtedly a useful technique for establishing an agricultural calendar in a dry and often unforgiving land. But the intensity of interest went far beyond that of agriculturists simply following the movement of the sun along the horizon.

The Anasazi paid attention to the heavens, but they did more. The picture that emerges is that of an astronomical infrastructure, consisting of people with skill, knowledge, and power.   Certain individuals had the techniques for determining accurate cardinal directions, the knowledge of the short and long cycles of sun and moon, and the political authority to influence major construction projects. There must also have been a persuasive belief system containing astronomical motifs which provided justification for such major endeavors as the construction of the Chimney Rock Pueblo and the alignments of the great kivas.

Furthermore, we appear to be encountering a highly tuned sense of the harmony of nature. Rituals expressive of such harmony apparently could not be casual affairs but had to be performed with accurate geographic orientation in order to be effective.  Both cosmology and cosmogony must have had roles.  Accurate cosmology is manifest in the attention to the alignment of human lives to the structure of the cosmos.  The cosmogonic re-enactments of the origins of the world may have involved rituals performed on the north-south roads of Chaco and Yellow Jacket and in the great kivas. Practical calendrics, in which the solar and lunar calendars were reconciled, may be manifest in the concern for midwinter fullmoon rise at Chimney Rock, the corner windows at Pueblo Bonito, and the sun room at Hovenweep Castle.

Moving throughout all of these activities are the shadowy figures of skilled practitioners, who perhaps traveled and traded their astronomical skills throughout the Anasazi culture area.  In the thirteenth century, their roles may have intensified or radically changed. Their skills may have been desperately sought or their reputations denigrated when the harmony between the earth and sun faltered, the sun acquired ugly spots on its surface, and the land began to fail as a provider.

# Seven

## Sunspots and Abandonment

The Greek concept of the perfection of the heavens led Galileo into trouble with the Church of Rome when he observed spots on the sun with his telescope in A.D. 1611. Objects in the sky, especially the sun, were supposed to be eternal and without blemish. Ironically, only a few decades after he observed them, sunspots began to disappear, and for nearly a hundred years sunspots were strangely absent from the sun's disk. This period of missing sunspots, known as the Maunder Minimum, lasted from 1630 through 1720.[1] During this period Europe experienced the so-called Little Ice Age, a time immortalized in many Christmas scenes of frozen canals in Holland and houses nearly buried under drifts of snow. During the Maunder Minimum the annual mean temperatures of Paris and London were 1° below normal, and ice formed regularly on the River Thames.

Galileo knew that sunspots were carried across the sun's disk by its 27-day rotation. More than two hundred years after the first telescopic observations of sunspots, their 11-year periodicity was discovered by Heinrich Schwabe[2] (Figure 1). Within recent years we have discovered that the temperature of the sun varies with the eleven year waxing and waning of the numbers of spots. When there are many spots on the sun's disk, it is warmer; at sunspot minimum it is cooler.

### The Medieval Maximum

Occasionally sunspots grow to such large size that they can be seen with the unaided eye (Figure 2). Observations of these naked-eye sunspots predate Galileo's observations by at least fifteen hundred years.[3] The most systematic observations of naked-eye sunspots come from the Orient which was free of the Greek insistence on the perfec-

$R_Z$

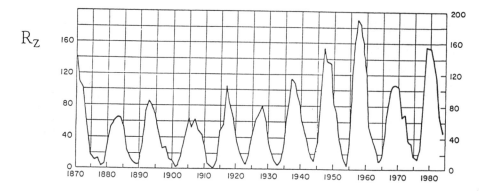

**Figure 1.** Sunspot numbers, $R_z$, from A.D. 1870 to 1985.

tion of the sun. The earliest reference to sunspots in the Orient is from 28 B.C.

The careful recording of naked-eye sunspots by the Chinese enables us to detect periods of unusually high sunspot activity. Naked-eye sunspots were abundant from A.D. 300 to 400 and from 500 to 579. By far the greatest outburst of naked eye sunspots occurred between 1100 and 1387, with a peak around 1200. This episode of extreme sunspot activity is now known as the Medieval Maximum.

The sun is not a constant provider. Sunspots come and go, and in response to the changes occurring on the sun, the climate of the earth changes over the centuries. The sun is .05% to .1% percent brighter at a typical sunspot maximum than at sunspot minimum. During the Medieval Maximum the output of energy from the sun may have been 1% greater than it is today, and the average temperature of the earth may have been raised by 1-2° Celsius.

The astronomer Andrew Douglas, originally working at the Lowell Observatory in Flagstaff, had hoped to find the history of the changing sun written in the rings of trees.[4] Since tree growth is an objective diary of local climate, and since climate should respond to solar activity, Douglas hoped to find an 11-year periodicity in tree rings that exactly matched the 11-year periodicity in sunspots. Douglas was able to use the variable width of the tree rings to establish a time sequence that could be used to date accurately the time at which the tree was cut. He also noted that the tree rings in the period between A. D 1276 and 1299 were unusually narrow, indicating a drought and/or a cold spell in the Southwest during that time.

In his searching for the 11-year cycle in the earth's weather, Douglas established the basic principles of the science of dendrochronology, which is now the most precise source of information about ancient cli-

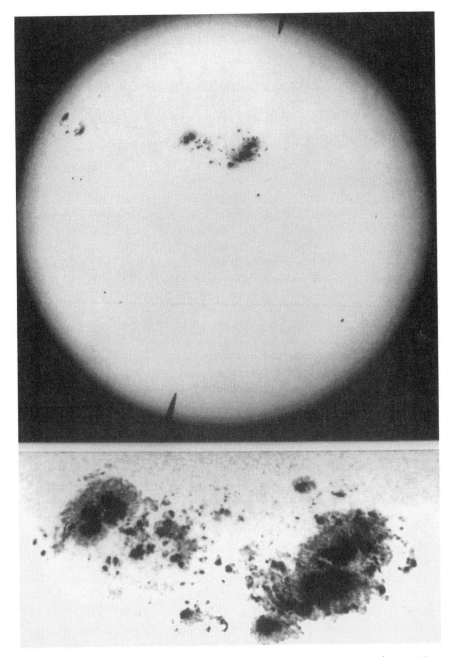

**Figure 2.**  One of the largest sunspots ever to be photographed, April 7, 1947.

mates in the Southwest. By identifying the date of the last tree ring before the tree was cut, individual ruins can be absolutely dated to the
year and, as we found at Chimney Rock, sometimes even to the season.
But when Douglas died at the age of 95 in 1962, he still had not provided
firm evidence for a direct, one-to-one link between the sun and weather
using tree rings. His legacy, his almost inadvertent gift to southwestern
archaeology, is the most accurate dating technique available.

Another technique used to explore the past history of solar activity
utilizes radioactive carbon, $C^{14}$, an unstable isotope with a half-life of
5730 years (Figure 3). Analysis of the varying abundance of $C^{14}$ provides additional evidence that something strange and unusual was
happening to the sun in the twelfth and thirteenth centuries.[5] Produced by the impact of high energy cosmic rays in the upper atmosphere of the earth, $C^{14}$ is anti-correlated with solar activity. When
sunspots are numerous, $C^{14}$ is diminished in the earth's atmosphere.
Cosmic rays are deflected by the outermost magnetic field of the sun,
which waxes and wanes with the 11 year cycle of solar activity. When
sunspots are very numerous on the sun, its magnetic field penetrates
deeply and strongly into the surrounding interplanetary space and
thereby shields the earth from cosmic rays. The production of $C^{14}$ is
thus diminished during periods of intense solar activity. The $C^{14}$ record
has provided confirmation of the Medieval Maximum as well as the
two recent minima of sun spots the Maunder Minimum and the Sporer
Minimum of A.D. 1400-1510. Further evidence for the intensification of
solar activity at the time of the Medieval Maximum is found in the
records of observations of aurora, which were especially abundant in
the the twelfth and thirteenth centuries.

Unstable climate patterns may have developed in Mesoamerica and
the Southwest. The Medieval Maximum saw major shifts of populations such as the Toltecs, Mexica, and Anasazi. There is strong evidence
that cultural dislocations in the Southwest were related to climatic
changes.

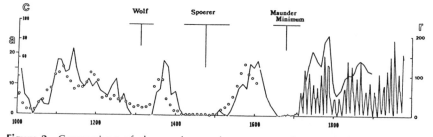

**Figure 3.** Comparison of observed annual sunspot numbers (r, scale at right) and
estimated sunspot numbers obtained from measurements of $C^{14}$ from tree rings
(c, fine line) and from observations of the aurora borealis (a, circles).

Another possible consequence of the Medieval Maximum emerges from the temple traditions of India. During the period from A.D. 500 to 1300 sun worship was a major activity in India, and many large temples dedicated to the sun were built.[6] One of the greatest temples ever built in India is in the form of a giant chariot of the sun, carried by 24 wheels, each representing a particular fortnight of the year, drawn to the east by seven great horses (Figure 4). This temple at Konarak, south of Calcutta, was started in A.D. 1240 at the height of the Medieval Maximum. The construction of the temple proceeded with strangely negative undertones, judging from local folk stories,[7] and when completed in A. D. 1258 it apparently never functioned as a major center of worship. Prior to the Medieval Maximum, the sun, in the form of the god, Surya, was placed on a level equal to that of the major deities of Hinduism, Vishnu and Shiva. The disk of the sun was described as the visible manifestation of the highest principle of reality. But strangely, following the Moslem invasion of north India in the thirteenth century, sun worship diminished in popularity, never to regain the influence it once had. Other sects of Hinduism that also experienced the destruction of their temples by the Moslem invaders recovered and flourished, but the sun never returned.

A possible explanation for the failure of sun worship is the shock of discovery of naked-eye sunspots. The pure and brilliant sun was not really so pure after all (Figure 5). The morning ritual of a greeting to the sun is performed by tens of thousands every morning of the year, many of them on the west bank of the River Ganges in the mists rising from the waters.[8] Could they possibly have missed those dark blotches moving across the face of the sun during the Medieval Maximum?

In some 70 temples of south India the festival known as *suryapuja* occurs when at sunrise, direct sunlight is able to enter the *garbha griha*, the sacred center of the temple, and touch the highly polished black stone of the Shiva lingam enshrined therein.[9] In most temples the event occurs during a few days near the equinoxes. Surprisingly, in this dramatic and important festival, the sun is not being worshiped, but rather the sun is understood to be prostrating himself, worshiping the deity of the temple. Furthermore, at a few temples the sun is understood to be cursed and suffering from leprosy and requests forgiveness from Lord Shiva and relief from his terrible affliction. Since elsewhere in India the sun is associated with purification and is invoked to cure leprosy, it is very curious that the sun is believed to be suffering from skin disease. The tradition of the leprous sun may have originated when the actual sun was suffering from an outbreak of spots during the Medieval Maximum.

There is another possible reference to a spotted sun which comes

**Figure 4.** Wheel of the chariot of the sun at Konarak, India.

**Figure 5.** Lotus once held by the sun god at Konarak, before the arms of the stat-
ue were hacked off by Moslem invaders. The lotus is illuminated by the first light
of the morning sun on the day of the sun's birthday, Magh Saptami. Gleaming
white, pure, and undefiled by its surroundings, the lotus is one of the primary
symbols of the sun in India.

from half-way around the world. In the Aztec creation mythology, after the fourth destruction of the world, the gods gathered in Teotihuacán to create the world for the fifth and last time. Around a fire burning on the summit of the Pyramid of the Sun, the Aztec gods prepared to create the Fifth Sun by the self-immolation of one of their members.[10] The god who first threw himself into the fire to become the sun was Nanahuatl, the Pimply One, the Ulcerated One, hideously disfigured by running sores which covered his entire body. It requires no great leap of the imagination to suspect that here again, buried in myth, is an acknowledgement of the trauma and puzzlement associated with the the abundance of naked eye sunspots during the Medieval Maximum.

Another possible tragic consequence of the outburst of sunspots has been recently suggested by John Eddy. We suspect that because of the increased temperature of the sun associated with heightened sunspot activity there would have been an increased amount of ultraviolet radiation reaching the surface of the earth, especially in the equatorial latitudes. There is evidence that malignant melanoma in humans follows the 11-year cycle of sunspot activity. Eddy suggests that a plague of fatal skin cancer may have broken out during the Medieval Maximum, destabilizing some cultures and causing them to abandon their homelands and move elsewhere. It may have been melanoma on human skin and not just spots on the sun which led the Hindus and the Mexica to associate leprosy and ulcers with the sun. The adoption by the Mexica of an angry and wrathful sun god may have been in response to the transformation of a benign sun into one associated with drought and disease.

## Abandonment

A poignant mystery has always been associated with the abandonment of the Anasazi homeland.[11] It is entirely possible that sunspots may have been related to the exodus of the Anasazi. They had abandoned their homes before as they moved in search of good farm land, game, and water. The duration of occupation of small sites was short. But the final abandonment of a such a large area, leaving it empty of people, is unique. Elsewhere on the planet there had always been migrations of people forced out of their homeland by population pressure and failing climates, but for a people to depart and leave no one behind is rare. In some of the ruins at Mesa Verde, the inhabitants seemingly intended to return, leaving cups, bowls, sandals, and other domestic items carefully arranged. Climate appears to have been the primary villain. As the populations increased, stimulated initially by a period of benign weather, there was a movement into larger communities and a consequent greater dependence on farming. Game would have become less plentiful in the vicinity of population centers. As the climate began to falter in the middle of the thirteenth century, the ability of the Anasazi to adapt to change was seriously reduced.

The political system of the settlements may have been inadequate to respond effectively to the climatic challenge. There may have been no leaders able to organize the society in such a period of stress. Though there were sun priests, they may have been discredited as the climate failed. The social structure of the community may have collapsed with the failure of the land and sun to provide. The northern Anasazi migrated eastward to settle among the populations living in the Rio Grande valley.

Recent studies of tree ring data from the Colorado Plateau indicate that there was a change in the frequency of droughts after A.D. 1150. Droughts may have become more frequent and of shorter duration. The strategies that had once been appropriate may not have been sufficient during the periods of frequent years of poor rainfall and poor harvests.

In the Four Corners Region there is clear and direct evidence of a serious climate change.[12] Pollen analysis and tree ring studies indicate that the region was hit by a devastating combination of drought and cold beginning approximately in A.D. 1200. A cooling trend would have narrowed the window of frost-free days, perhaps reducing it below the approximately 80 days needed for cultivation of aboriginal corn. At that time there was apparently a sudden change to cold and dry weather that continued for 600 years.

Between A.D. 800 and 1050, the climate in the Four Corners area was apparently as wet as the present but cooler; between 1050 and 1150 it was as wet and warm as the present. Then following 1250 a major climatic change occurred, and the region entered a dry and cold period which lasted until the beginning of the present century. Visitors in 1859 described the Mancos and Dolores regions as dry and sterile.

*Sage is the predominant vegetation, and no water is found . . . yet we passed several ruined buildings, and broken pottery is scattered everywhere. Surouaro is the name of a ruined town which must once have contained a population of several thousands. The name is said to be of Indian (Utah) origin, and to signify desolation, and certainly no better could have been selected. The surrounding country is hopelessly sterile; and, whatever it once may have been, Surouaro is now desolate enough . . . but where a population of many thousands once existed, now as many hundreds could not be sustained, either by agriculture or the chase. The surrounding country contains very little animal life, and almost none of it is now cultivable. It is 7000 feet in al-*

*titude, intensely cold in winter and very dry throughout the year. The want of water alone would forbid the residence of any considerable number of persons at Surouaro if everything else were furnished them. The arroyos, through which streams seem to have once flowed, are now dry, and it was only with great difficulty that sufficient water was obtained for the supply of our train. The remains of metates are abundant in the ruins, and corn was doubtless the staple article of their existence, but none could be raised here . . . and the readiest solution of the problem would to infer a change in climate, by which this region was made uninhabitable.*[13]

One result of climate change occurring in the thirteenth century could have been a preoccupation with events in the skies. The sun must have been watched closely for good or bad omens to determine whether or not it was to be a good agricultural year. A series of bad years of drought and early, killing frosts would have intensified ritual activity connected with the sun.

Much of what drove the Anasazi astronomer may thus have been stimulated by the unstable climate associated with the Medieval Maximum of sunspot activity. We can speculate on the thoughts of the sun priests, observing the sun through the morning mists with puzzlement and horror. Ominous black spots crawled across its surface, the land was cold and dry, and society was falling apart. The dark side of Father Sun had asserted itself, and beneath the flecked sun the people said, "we must flee."

# Eight

## The Sun Temple of Mesa Verde

Few visitors to Mesa Verde National Park miss the opportunity to explore the Sun Temple, and few leave that extraordinary structure without a mixture of admiration for its builders and puzzlement over its meaning. With its careful design and symmetry, it is clearly not a purposeless or unplanned building.

When he excavated the building in 1915, Jessie Fewkes concluded that it must have been primarily dedicated to ceremonial activities.[1] The effort expended in pecking and shaping nearly every stone of the wall veneer indicated the importance of the building for the people who lived in its vicinity. Built on a narrow peninsula, the Sun Temple is bordered by Cliff Canyon to the north and Fewkes Canyon to the south. In the Cliff and Fewkes canyon area are some 33 habitation sites, including Cliff Palace, Oak Tree House, Fire Temple, Mummy House, and Sunset House.[2] With a total of some 530 rooms and 60 kivas, the population in the vicinity of the Sun Temple may have exceeded 600.

During the summer of 1991, we found evidence of a horizon calendar that could have been used by observers in Cliff Palace.[3] We had been encouraged in our search by ethnographic analogy with the Pueblo culture, for at least 19 of the 24 historic Pueblo communities had one or more members who practiced sun-watching near the times of solstices for the purpose of establishing an agricultural and festival calendar.[4] As noted in Chapter Three, the standard technique among the Pueblos was to observe the position of the rising or setting sun relative to irregularities of the horizon from an observing station inside or close to a settlement. The most important solar festival among the historic Pueblos was winter solstice, a time when there was sometimes concern that the sun would be delayed in its return to the north unless appropriate ceremonies were performed.

Cliff Palace faces a southwestern horizon where the sun sets on December 21, the evening of winter solstice. But, today, the horizon is a nearly flat expanse devoid of major natural markers. The one object that breaks the horizon is the Sun Temple on the opposite mesa at a distance of 288 meters across Cliff Canyon. Where would an Anasazi watcher have stood to observe winter solstice sunset over the Sun Temple? At the extreme southern end of Cliff Palace we discovered a small level platform containing a circular basin pecked in the bedrock with a diameter of 8 cm. and a depth of 3 cm. (Figure 1). When one stands over the pecked basin, the perimeter wall of the Sun Temple has an altitude of nearly 5°. The center of the Sun Temple (half-way between its two circular rooms) has an azimuth of 235°24' (Figure 2). Taking into account the effect of atmospheric refraction, we estimate the lower limb of the winter solstice sun would have touched the top edge of the perimeter wall of the Sun Temple at an azimuth of approximately 235°18'. Thus it appears that the Sun Temple may have been built, at least partially, to serve as an artificial horizon marker for winter solstice.

Among the historic Pueblos there was a distinction between offertory shrines to the sun and calendrical sun-watching stations.[4] The pecked basin may have marked a sun-watching station while the strangely eroded rock at the southwest corner of the Sun Temple may have been an offertory shrine. The offertory shrines were often associated with unusual stones, concretions, or oddly shaped rocks such as the one contained in the stone enclosure. Such shrines were sites, usually some distance from the pueblo, where water, corn meal, prayer sticks, or prayer feathers were placed. The line connecting the pecked basin to this possible offertory shrine for the sun has an azimuth of 235°50', also notably close to that of the setting winter solstice sun (Figure 2).

There is a second potential line-of-sight across the Sun Temple established by the tangent to its two circular rooms. That tangent line falls upon the center of the prominent four-story tower of Cliff Palace and may identify a foresight visible to an observer in the third or fourth story of the tower. If the two circular rooms of the Sun Temple had been towers extending above its perimeter wall, they could have functioned as a "gunsight" for an observer in the four-story tower. The line-of-sight from the center of the T-shaped doorway in the fourth story through the gap formed by the double towers has an azimuth of 227°2'. The sun never reaches that far south, but the moon at major southern standstill would have touched the perimeter wall of the Sun Temple at an azimuth of 227°9' and thus would have fitted nicely in the gap between the towers every 18.6 years (Figures 2 & 3).

The intersection of the lunar standstill line-of-sight with the square tower is particularly significant because pictographs painted on its

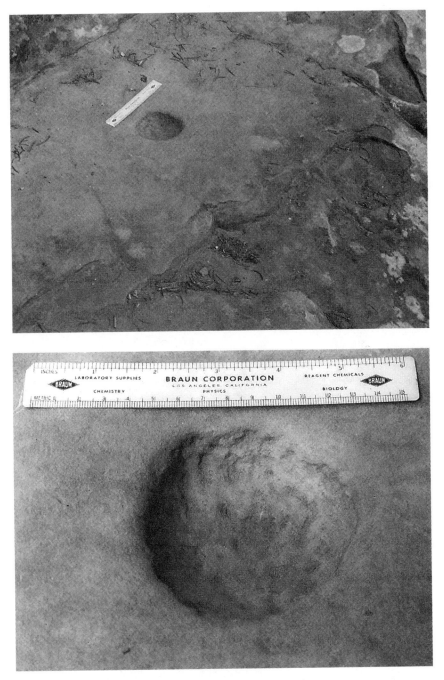

**Figure 1.** Pecked basin in Cliff Palace

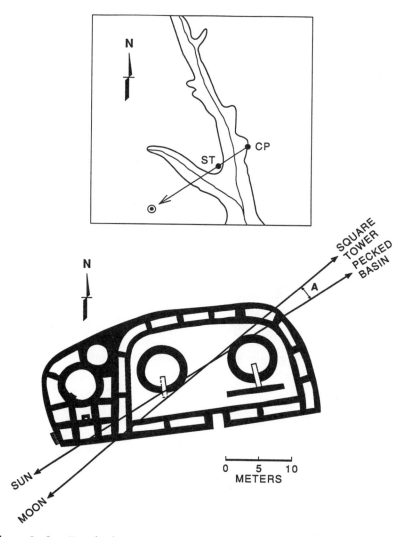

**Figure 2.** Sun Temple showing the two sight-lines to sunset at winter solstice and to moonset at major southern standstill. ST, Sun Temple; CP, Cliff Palace. A=8°22'.

interior walls, some of the finest pictographs in the park, may be associated with the moon. On the interior wall of the third story of the tower there are four vertical lines each containing 17–20 tick marks, appearing more like tally marks of events than decorative designs (Figure 4). The total number of such marks is 74–75, corresponding to an average of 18.5–18.75; these marks may be records of four lunar standstill cycles observed from Cliff Palace. Tree ring dates in the Cliff-Fewkes Canyon area span the time period between A.D. 1180–1279. The

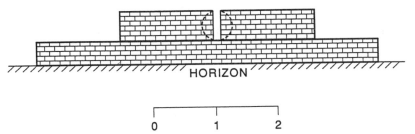

**Figure 3.** Possible appearance of the twin towers of Sun Temple as viewed from Cliff Palace. The size of the moon as it might have appeared in the gap is shown.

exact dates of initial habitation and final abandonment are unknown, but four major standstill cycles could have been observed at 18.6-year intervals from Cliff Palace starting with the standstill of A.D. 1187 and continuing through the standstill of A.D. 1280.

A second pictograph that may also have a lunar association is found at approximately the same height as the four lines (Figure 5). Contained within a rectangular border, the figure is divided by a vertical line with approximately twelve marks and on either side there are twelve zigzags. Such a pattern is not uncommon in Anasazi art, but the recurrence of twelve marks and twelve zigzags is noteworthy because of the twelve "moons" during the year. In one month, the moon swings from southern extreme to northern extreme and back to southern extreme. That pictograph may be a representation of the changing positions of the rising and setting moons during a one-year period. It is the kind of diagram that an astronomer of today might draw on a blackboard to illustrate the changing positions of the moon or an Anasazi astronomer might have drawn for an apprentice.

Immediately beneath the rectangle is a third pictograph consisting of two sets of three triangles separated by twelve circles (Figure 6). The triangles may represent the La Plata Peaks on the northeastern horizon and the circles may represent an annual series of sunrises or moonrises.

We cannot know for certain what was in the mind of the artist or artists who painted these pictographs. But the correspondences are impressive: they are located at the third floor of the tower where an observer could view the setting moon over the Sun Temple; they contain numbers corresponding to the lunar cycles of 12 months and 18.6 years; and, finally, the observing location in the tower is on the tangent line of the circular rooms of Sun Temple which intersects the setting moon at major southern standstill.

Initially a more modest structure, perhaps nothing more than a pile of rocks, may have been built on the location of the Sun Temple to

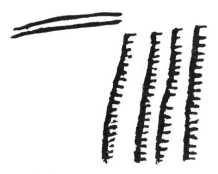

**Figure 4.** Four sets of tick marks in the four-story tower of Cliff Palace.

**Figure 5.** Pictographs in the four-story tower of Cliff Palace.

serve as a solstice marker for an observer standing at the pecked basin. The site may have gradually evolved into a carefully constructed astronomical sighting device, a solar-lunar shrine, and an important ceremonial structure for the Cliff-Fewkes Canyon community.

Ethnography of historic Pueblos indicates that the ability to predict and anticipate the date of winter or summer solstice is as important as the confirmation of the event.[3] The nearly perfect symmetry of the Sun Temple is broken by an addition, which Fewkes described as the

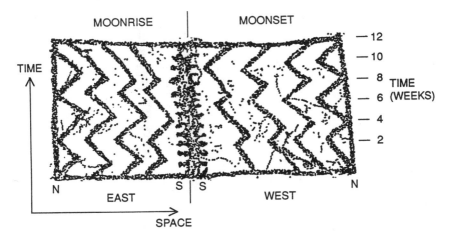

**Figure 6.** Possible representation of the
varying positions of the moon on the horizon.

"Annex," on its northwest side consisting of an additional circular room and a smaller circular structure which may have been a tower. As seen from the pecked basin the sun sets over the center of the tower on approximately December 2–3, providing thereby a twenty-day warning before winter solstice.

The experience at Cliff Palace of watching the moon set between double towers at the Sun Temple is reminiscent of the similar situation at Chimney Rock described in Chapter Five. Could it be that the inhabitants of Cliff Palace were intentionally duplicating the experience of the moon rising between the double pinnacles of Chimney Rock?

Around the time of major standstill, the moon would have appeared in a dark sky in the gap between the towers only during the spring in the six-month period between winter solstice and summer solstice. The moon would have first appeared in the gap after winter solstice as a slender crescent. Month by month, with impressive regularity, the moon in the gap would have grown in size, until the full moon would have set at sunrise near the day of summer solstice.

The rotation of the east-west axis of the Sun Temple by some 10° away from cardinality may also have an astronomical explanation. The architectural precision of the Sun Temple suggests that a departure from true east-west may not have been accidental or arbitrary. A clue to this puzzle may be provided by a second, large pecked basin five meters north of the Sun Temple. The basin lies on the perpendicular drawn from the southern wall and may indicate an important direction to the north. Standing above the alcove in the southern wall, looking across the center of the Sun Temple and across the basin beyond, one faces the direction of

Cedar Tree Tower some two kilometers to the north. The tower is built of double-coursed walls in which the stones have been carefully pecked to fit the curvature of the walls. It is similar in the quality of its construction to the Sun Temple, and contains a third pecked basin in its bedrock floor which may mark a second sun-watching station.

The northeastern horizon contains the prominent and sharp peaks of the La Platas, which would have provided excellent calendrical marks for summer solstice sunrise and lunar standstill. Announcement of the dates of ceremonies determined from observations of the sun on the horizon may have been visually communicated by fires from the Cedar Tree Tower southward to the Sun Temple and northward to the Far View community, perhaps to Far View Tower.

Astronomical ceremonies associated with both sun and moon may have occurred at the Sun Temple, Cliff Palace, and Cedar Tree Tower. The orientation of the Sun Temple to the Cedar Tree Tower may have had an important ritual significance if celebrants standing in the Sun Temple could have seen signal fires originating at the Cedar Tree Tower announcing the times of important events. Participants in a winter solstice festival in Cliff Palace could have watched the sun at winter solstice setting over the Sun Temple. They may have been impressed by such a demonstration of the order of the heavens and of the power of individuals to identify and predict that order.

# NOTES

Chapter 1: The Anasazi Astronomer

1. Frank Waters, *The Book of the Hopi*, Viking Press, New York, pp. 3-28, 1963.
2. Stella Kramrisch, *The Hindu Temple*, University of Calcutta, 1946.
3. Johanna Broda, David Carrasco, and Eduardo Matos Moctezuma, *The Great Temple of Tenochtitlán, Center and Periphery in the Aztec World*, University of California Press, Berkeley, 1987.
4. J. McKim Malville, "Prehistoric Astronomy in the American Southwest," *The Astronomy Quarterly*, 8, 1-36, 1991.
5. J. McKim Malville, "Astronomy and Social Integration Among the Anasazi," *Proceedings of the Anasazi Symposium, 1991*, ed. Art Hutchinson and Jack E. Smith, Mesa Verde Museum Association, 1993.
6. W. James Judge, "Chaco: Current Views of Prehistory and the Regional System" in *Chaco and Hohokam*, ed. Patricia L. Crown and W. James Judge, School of American Research Press, Santa Fe, pp. 11-30, 1991.
7. J. McKim Malville, Frank Eddy and Carol Ambruster, "Lunar Standstills at Chimney Rock," *Archaeoastronomy*, Supplement to the *Journal for the History of Science* 16, S43-S50, 1991;
J. McKim Malville "Chimney Rock and the Moon: The Shrine at the Edge of the World," in *The Chimney Rock Symposium*, ed. J. McKim Malville and Gary Matlock, Rocky Mountain Forest and Range Experiment Station, U.S. Forest Service, Fort Collins, 1993.
8. Lewis Binford, "Smudge pits and hide smoking: the use of analogy in archaeological reasoning," *American Antiquity*, 32, 1-12, 1967.

Chapter 2: The Dome of the Sky

1. Linda S. Cordell, *Prehistory of the Southwest*, Academic Press, New York, 1984.
2. Matthew W. Stirling, "Origin Myth of Acoma," *Bureau of American Ethnology Bulletin* 135:1-123, Smithsonian Institution, Washington, D.C.
3. Ray A. Williamson, "Light and Shadow, Ritual, and Astronomy in Anasazi Structures," in *Astronomy and Ceremony in the Prehistoric Southwest*, ed. John B. Carlson and W. James Judge, Papers of the Maxwell Museum of Anthropology, Number 2, Albuquerque, 1983, pp. 99-119.
4. Linda S. Cordell, *Prehistory of the Southwest*, p. 254. *op. cit.*
5. Stephen H. Lekson, *Great Pueblo Architecture of Chaco Canyon*, University of New Mexico Press, Albuquerque, 1986.
6. Ray A. Williamson, "Casa Rinconada, a Twelfth Century Anasazi Kiva," in *Archaeoastronomy in the New World*, ed. Anthony F. Aveni, Cambridge University Press, Cambridge, England, 1982, pp. 205-219.
7. Michael Zeilik, "The Ethnoastronomy of the Historic Pueblos: Calendrical Sun Watching," *Archaeoastronomy*, Supplement to the *Journal for the History of Astronomy* 8 (1985): 1-24.
8. Florence H. Ellis, "A Thousand Years of the Pueblo Sun-moon-star Calendar," in *Archaeoastronomy in Precolumbian America*, ed. A. F. Aveni, University of Texas, Austin, 1975, pp. 59-87.

9. Ray Norris, "Megalithic Observatories in Britain: Real or Imagined?" in *Records in Stone, Papers in Memory of Alexander Thom*, ed. C.L.N. Ruggles, Cambridge University Press, Cambridge, 1988, pp. 262-276.

Chapter 3: Skywatchers

1. Michael Zeilik, "Sun Shrines and Sun Symbols in the U.S. Southwest," *Archaeoastronomy*, Supplement to the *Journal for the History of Astronomy* 16 (1985): S86-S96. Michael Zeilik, "The Ethnoastronomy of the Historic Pueblos, I: Calendrical Sun Watching," *Archaeoastronomy*, Supplement to the *Journal for the History of Astronomy* 16 (1985): S1-S24.
2. Frank Hamilton Cushing, "My Adventures in Zuni," in *Zuni: The Selected Writings of Frank Hamilton Cushing*, ed. J. Green, University of Nebraska Press, Lincoln, 1979, pp. 116-117.
3. Michael Zeilik, "The Ethnoastronomy of the Historic Pueblos, I: Sun Watching." *op. cit.*
4. Stephen C. McCluskey, "Historical Archaeoastronomy: The Hopi Example," in *Archaeoastronomy in the New World*, ed. A.F. Aveni, Cambridge University Press, 1982, pp. 31-57.
5. Michael Zeilik, "The Ethnoastronomy of the Historical Pueblos, I: Sun Watching." *op. cit.*
6. Alfonso Ortiz, *The Tewa World: Space Time, Being and Becoming in a Pueblo Society*, University of Chicago Press, Chicago, 1969.
7. Michael Zeilik, "The Ethnoastronomy of the Historic Pueblos, II: Moon Watching," *Archaeoastronomy*, Supplement to the *Journal for the History of Astronomy* 17 (1986): S1-S22.
8. Florence H. Ellis, "A Thousand Years of the Pueblo Sun-Moon-Star Calendar," in *Archaeoastronomy in Precolumbian America*, ed. A. F. Aveni, University of Texas, Austin, 1975, pp. 59-87.
9. Michael Zeilik, "The Ethnoastronomy of the Historic Pueblos, II: Moon Watching." *op. cit.*
10. Barbara Tedlock, "Zuni Sacred Theater," *American Indian Quarterly* 7:93-109.
11. Michael Zeilik, "The Ethnoastronomy of the Historic Pueblos, II: Moon Watching." *op. cit.*
12. Ibid.
13. Barbara Tedlock, "Zuni Sacred Theater." *op. cit.*; Michael Zeilik, "The Ethnoastronomy of the Historic Pueblos, II: Moon Watching." *op. cit.*
14. Florence Hawley Ellis, "A Thousand Years of the Pueblo Sun-Moon-Star Calendar," *op. cit.*
15. Ibid.

Chapter 4: Chaco Canyon and Hovenweep

1. David G. Nobel, ed., *New Light on Chaco Canyon*, School of American Research, Santa Fe, 1984.
2. Chris Kincaid, ed., *Chaco Roads Project*, Phase I. Bureau of Land Management, Santa Fe, 1983; Stephen Lekson, *Great Pueblo Architecture of Chaco Canyon*, University of New Mexico Press, Albuquerque, New Mexico, 1986.
3. Anna P. Sofaer and Rolf M. Sinclair, "Astronomical Markings at Three Sites on Fajada Butte"; Michael Zeilik, "Anticipation in Ceremony: The

Readiness is All"; John B. Carlson, "Romancing the Stone, or Moonshine on the Sun Dagger"; in *Astronomy and Ceremony in the Prehistoric Southwest*, Papers of the Maxwell Museum of Anthropology, Number 2, Albuquerque 1987, pp. 25-88.

4. Michael Zeilik, "The Fajada Butte Solar Marker: A Reevaluation," *Science* 228 (1985):1311-1313.

5. Ray A. Williamson, *Living the Sky*, Houghton Mifflin, Boston, 1984.

6. Michael Zeilik, "The Sun Watchers of Chaco Canyon," *Griffith Observer* 47 (1983): 2-12.

7. Johnathan E. Reyman, "Astronomy, Architecture, and Adaptation at Pueblo Bonito," *Science* 193 (1976): 957-962; Ray A. Williamson, Howard J. Fisher, and Donnel O'Flynn, "Anasazi Solar Observations," in *Native American Astronomy*, ed. A. F. Aveni, University of Texas Press, Austin, 1977, pp. 203-217; Michael Zeilik, "Keeping a Seasonal Calendar at Pueblo Bonito," *Archaeoastronomy* 9 (1986): 79-87.

8. Ray A. Williamson, "Casa Rinconada, Twelfth Century Anasazi Kiva," in *Archaeoastronomy in the New World*, ed. A. F. Aveni, Cambridge University Press, Cambridge, 1982, pp. 205-219.

9. Frank Hamilton Cushing, "My Adventures in Zuni," in *Zuni: Selected Writings of Frank Hamilton Cushing*, ed. J. Green, University of Nebraska Press, Lincoln, 1979, pp. 116-117.

10. John C. Brandt, S.P. Maran, R. A. Williamson, R.S. Harrington, C. Cochran, M. Kennedy, W.J. Kennedy, and V.D. Chamberlain, "Possible Rock Art Records of the Crab Nebula Supernova in the Western United States," *Archaeoastronomy in Pre-Columbian America*, ed. A. F. Aveni, University of Texas Press, Austin, 1975, pp. 45-57.

11. Ray A. Williamson, *Living the Sky*, Houghton Mifflin, Boston, 1984.

12. Joseph C. Winter, "Hovenweep Through Time," in *Exploration*, ed. David G. Noble, School of American Research, Santa Fe, 1985, pp. 22-28.

13. Ray A. Williamson, Howard J. Fisher, and Donnel O'Flynn, "Anasazi Solar Observatories," in *Native American Astronomy*, ed. Anthony F. Aveni, University of Texas Press, Austin, 1977, pp. 203-217; Michael Zeilik, "Anticipation in Ceremony: The Readiness Is All." *op. cit.*; Ray A. Williamson, "Light and Shadow, Ritual and Astronomy in Anasazi Structures," in *Astronomy and Ceremony in the Prehistoric Southwest*, Papers of the Maxwell Museum of Anthropology, Number 2, Albuquerque, 1986, pp. 99-119.

14. Frank Hamilton Cushing, "My Adventures in Zuni." *op. cit.*

15. Ray A. Williamson, "Light and Shadow, Ritual and Astronomy in Anasazi Structures." *op. cit.*

16. Ibid.

Chapter 5: Moonrise and Sunrise Over Chimney Rock

1. F. W. Eddy, *Archaeological Investigations at Chimney Rock Mesa: 1970-1972*, Colorado Archaeological Society, Boulder, 1977; L. D. Webster, *An Archaeological Survey of the West Rim of the Piedra River*, San Juan National Forest, Durango, Colorado, 1983.

2. F. H. Ellis, "Differential Pueblo Specialization in Fetishes and Shrines," *Anales* 1967-1968, Sobretiro, Septima epoca, Tomo I, Mexico; F. H. Ellis and J. J. Brody, "Ceramic Stratigraphy and Tribal History at Taos Pueblo," *American Antiquity* 29 (1964): 3.

3. R. P. Powers, W. B. Gillespie, and S. H. Lekson, *The Outlier Survey: A Regional View of Settlement in the San Juan Basin*, Division of Cultural Research, National Park Service, Albuquerque, 1983.

4. S. W. Lekson, *Great Pueblo Architecture of Chaco Canyon*, University of New Mexico Press, Albuquerque, 1984.

5. R. G. Vivian, "An Inquiry into Prehistoric Social Organization in Chaco Canyon, New Mexico," in *Reconstructing Prehistoric Pueblo Societies*, ed. W. A. Longacre, University of New Mexico Press, Albuquerque, 1970, pp. 59-83.

6. M. Zeilik, "The Ethnoastronomy of the Historic Pueblos, II: Moon Watching," *Archaeoastronomy*, Supplement to the *Journal for the History of Astronomy* 10 (1986): S1-22.

7. F. H. Ellis and L. Hammack, "The Inner Sanctum of Feather Cave, a Mogollon Sun and Earth Shrine Linking Mexico and the Southwest," *American Antiquity* 30 (1968): 25.

8. A. Sofaer, A. V. Zinser, and R. M. Sinclair, "A Unique Solar Marking Construct," *Science* 206 (1979): 283-291; A. Sofaer, R. M. Sinclair, and L. E. Doggett, "Lunar Markings on Fajada Butte, Chaco Canyon, New Mexico," in *Archaeoastronomy in the New World*, ed. A.F. Aveni, Cambridge University Press, Cambridge, 1982, pp. 169-181.

9. Anthony F. Aveni, "Archaeoastronomy in the Southwestern United States: A Neighbor's Eye View," in *Astronomy and Ceremony in the Prehistoric Southwest*, ed. J. B. Carlson and W. James Judge, Maxwell Museum, Albuquerque, 1987, pp. 9-23; John B. Carlson, "Romancing the Stone, or Moonshine on the Sun Dagger," in *Astronomy and Ceremony in the Prehistoric Southwest*, ed. J. B. Carlson and W. James Judge, Maxwell Museum, Albuquerque, 1987, pp. 71-88; Michael Zeilk, "A Reassessment of the Fajada Butte Solar Marker," *Archaeoastronomy*, Supplement to the *Journal for the History of Astronomy* 16 (1985): S69-S85.

10. T. C. Windes, *Stone Circles of Chaco Canyon*, National Park Service, Albuquerque, 1978.

11. L. D. Webster, "An Archaeological Survey of the West Rim of the Piedra River." *op. cit.*

Chapter 6: The Yellow Jacket Ruin

1. Arthur Rohn, "Prehistoric Development in the Mesa Verde Region," in *Exploration*, ed. David G. Noble, School of American Research, Santa Fe, 1985, pp. 3-10.

2. Paul Wheatley, *The Pivot of the Four Quarters*, Aldine Publishing, Chicago, 1971.

3. Frederick Lange, Nancy Mahaney, Joe Ben Wheat, and Mark L. Chenault, *Yellow Jacket: A Four Corners Anasazi Ceremonial Center*, Johnson Books, Boulder, 1986

4. M. Zeilik, "Sun Shrines and Sun Symbols in the U.S. Southwest," *Archaeoastronomy*, Supplement to the *Journal for the History of Astronomy* 15 (1985): 86-96.

5. Edgar Hewett, *Pajarito Plateau and its Ancient People*, University of New Mexico Press, Albuquerque, 1938.

6. F. H. Ellis and L. Hammack, "The Inner Sanctum of Feather Cave, A Mogollon Sun and Earth Shrine Linking Mexico and the Southwest," *American Antiquity* 33 (1968): 25-44.

7. Doris Heyden, "Caves, Gods and Myths: World-View and Planning in Teotihuacán," in *Mesoamerican Sites and World Views*, ed. Elizabeth Benson, Dumbarton Oaks, Washington, D.C., 1981.

8. Broda, Johanna, "Templo Mayor as Ritual Space," in *The Great Temple of Tenochtitlán*, University of California, Berkeley, 1987, pp. 61-123.

9. Florence H. Ellis, "A Thousand Years of the Pueblo Sun-Moon-Star Calendar," in *Archaeoastronomy in Precolumbian America*, ed. A. F. Aveni, University of Texas, Austin, 1975, pp. 59-87.

10. A.F. Aveni, S.L. Gibbs, and H. Hartung, "The Caracol Tower at Chichén Itzá: An ancient astronomical observatory?" *Science* 188 (1975): 977-985.

11. Stephen H. Lekson, *Great Pueblo Architecture of Chaco Canyon*, New Mexico, University of New Mexico Press, Albuquerque, 1986.

12. Anna Sofar and Rolf Sinclair, "Cosmographic Expression in the Road System of the Chaco Culture of Northwestern New Mexico," *Proceedings of the Second Oxford Conference on Archaeoastronomy*, in press.

13. A. Ortiz, *The Tewa World: Space, Time, Being and Becoming in a Pueblo Society*, University of Chicago Press, Chicago, 1969.

14. R. T. Zuidema, The Ceque System of Cuzco, E. J. Brill, Leiden, 1964; "The Inca Calendar," in *Native American Astronomy*, ed. Anthony F. Aveni, University of Texas Press, Austin and London, 1977, pp. 219-259.

Chapter 7: Sunspots and Abandonment

1. John A. Eddy, "The Maunder Minimum," *Science* 192 (1976): 1189-1201.

2. R. J. Bray and R. E. Loughhead, *Sunspots*, John Wiley and Sons, New York, 1965; Robert W. Noyes, *The Sun, Our Star*, Harvard University Press, Cambridge, 1982.

3. F. Richard Stephenson and David H. Clark, *Applications of Early Astronomical Records*, Oxford University Press, New York, 1978.

4. John A. Eddy, "Historical and Arboreal Evidence for a Changing Sun," in *The New Solar Physics*, Westview Press, Boulder, 1978.

5. John A. Eddy, "The Maunder Minimum." *op. cit.*

6. Lalta Prasad Pandey, *Sun Worship in Ancient India*, Motilal Banarsidass, Delhi, 1971; V. C. Srivastava, *Sun-worship in Ancient India*, Indological Publications, Allahabad, 1972.

7. J. McKim Malville, "The Rise and Fall of the Sun Temple of Konarak: The Icon Versus the Morning Sun," *World Archaeoastronomy*, ed. Anthony F. Aveni, Cambridge University Press, 1989, pp. 377-388.

8. J. McKim Malville, "Sun Worship in Contemporary India," *Man in India* 65 (1985): 207-233.

9. J. McKim Malville, "Solar Hierophanies of South India," *Proceedings of the First International Conference in Ethnoastronomy*, ed. Von Del Chamberlain and M. Jane Young, in press.

10. Burr Cartwright Brundage, *The Fifth Sun*, University of Texas Press, Austin, 1979.

11. Linda Cordell, *Prehistory of the Southwest*, Academic Press, New York, 1984, pp. 303-327.

12. Kenneth Lee Peterson, "Climatic Reconstruction for the Dolores Project Area," *Dolores Archaeological Project: Studies in Environmental Archaeology*, U. S. Department of the Interior, Bureau of Reclamation, 1985.

13. J. S. Newberry, *Geological Report: In report of the exploring expedition from Santa Fe, New Mexico, to the junction of the Grand and Green rivers of the Great Colorado of the West, in 1859, under the command of Capt. J. N. Macomb, Corps of Topographical Engineers*, Government Printing Office, Washington D.C., 1876, pp. 9-118.

Chapter 8: The Sun Temple of Mesa Verde

1. J. W. Fewkes, *Art and Archaeology*, 3,341 (1916); *Excavation and Repair of Sun Temple, Mesa Verde National Park*, Department of the Interior, Washington (1916).
2. A. H. Rohn, *Cultural Change and Continuity on Chapin Mesa*, Regents Press, Lawrence, Kansas, 1977.
3. J. McKim Malville, "Astronomy and Social Integration Among the Anasazi," *Proceedings of the Anasazi Symposium, 1991*, ed. A. Hutchinson and J. E. Smith, Mesa Verde Museum Association, 1993.
4. M. Zeilik, *Archaeoastronomy*, Supplement to the *Journal for the History of Astronomy* 8: S1; M. Zeilik, *Archaeoastronomy* Supplement to the *Journal for the History of Astronomy* 9, S86 (1985); M. Zeilik, *Archaeoastronomy IX*, 79-87, (1986); M. Zeilik, *World Archaeoastronomy*, ed. A. F. Aveni, Cambridge University Press, Cambridge, 1989.

# CREDITS

Chapter 2:

1. a. James Walton
   b. J. McKim Malville
2. Snowdon Hodges
5. William K. Hartman, *Astronomy: The Cosmic Journey*, Wadsworth Publishing Co., Belmont, California, 1978.
6. John Lubs, Griffith Observatory
10. After C. Daryll Forde, "Hopi Agriculture and Land Ownership," *Journal of the Royal Anthropological Institute of Great Britain and Ireland* 61, pp. 357-405, 1931.
11. After E.C. Krupp, *In Search of Ancient Astonomies*, ed. E.C. Krupp, McGraw-Hill, New York, 1978.


Chapter 4:

1. After Stephen H. Lekson, Thomas C. Windes, John R. Stein, and W. James Judge, "The Chaco Canyon Community," *Scientific American*, July 1988, pp. 100-109.
2. a. Jean Kindig
   b. After Anna P. Sofaer and Rolf M. Sinclair, "Astronomical Markings at Three Sites on Fajada Butte," in *Astronomy and Ceremony in the Prehistoric Southwest*, ed. John B. Carlson and W. James Judge, Maxwell Museum of Anthropology, Albuquerque, 1987.
3. Stephen H. Lekson, *Great Pueblo Architecture of Chaco Canyon, New Mexico*, Univeristy of New Mexico Press, Albuquerque, 1987.
4. After Ray W. Williamson, "Casa Rinconada, A Twelfth Century Anasazi Kiva," in *Archaeoastronomy in the New World*, ed. A.F. Aveni, Cambridge University Press, Cambridge, 1982, pp. 205-219.
5. Jean Kindig
6. J. McKim Malville
7. Michael Zeilik
8. J. McKim Malville


Chapter 5:

1. Frank Eddy
2. a. Dale Lightfoot
   b. Frank Eddy

Chapter 6:

1. a.  Jean Kindig
   b.  Jean Kindig
3. Jean Kindig
4. Jean Kindig
5. J. McKim Malville
6. J. McKim Malville
7. J. McKim Malville
9. Rudy Poglitsh
10. b.  Jean Kindig


Chapter 7:

1. John A. Eddy
2. Mt. Wilson Observatory
3. John A. Eddy
4. J. McKim Malville
5. J. McKim Malville


Chapter 8:

1. J. McKim Malville

# INDEX